TO RESTORE AMERICAN LIBERTY

A 21st Century Patriot's Declaration of Personal Independence.
His Prescription: Privitization

BY GEORGE J. HEIDEMAN
Centenarian, Patriot

PUBLISHED BY
NATIONAL LEGAL AND POLICY CENTER

Copyright © 2014 George J. Heideman

ISBN: 0615983529
ISBN 13: 9780615983523

Dedicated To

The Urgent Pursuit of
Life, Liberty and Righteousness.

FOREWORD

by Peter Flaherty

Why should anybody read a book by an unknown author? It has a "heavy" title, and reads like a textbook! But it is about that which is of vital importance to all of us—our way of life, and how that can be improved.

It is factually based, its conclusions are well reasoned. They are not based on partisanship or emotions. Its solid philosophy goes back to our ancient roots based on the unchanged nature of modern man. Like a textbook, it is wordy and at times repetitive, all in an effort to make the student-reader understand.

There are four reasons you should read this book — curiosity, history, patriotism and a self-help book to help achieve the American Dream.

Curiosity. What could an unknown author over 100 years old possibly have to say? Is it senility setting in or is it well-reasoned wisdom gathered through many decades?

History. The author has lived for over 100 years in a nation that is only 237 years old. History is frequently varied in its telling, often more interesting and illuminating. Perhaps this ancient author can do that for us. He grew up on a farm in Illinois, and his family was the second to own this property since President Polk signed the deed in 1847. Since his birth in 1912, he has seen much of the history of this nation unfold. He had an active and successful academic, professional and business career, and never "retired."

Patriotism. He was always a solid, law-abiding citizen. Drafted before Pearl Harbor, he served over five years in the service, from private to Commander in the United States Navy. In serving this country, he followed the actions of his ancestors. His grandfather fought the Sioux in Minnesota and then the Confederates in the south. And before that, his great grandfather helped defeat Napoleon at Waterloo in June of 1815.

A self-help book to help achieve the American Dream. Books remain one of the most important communicators of ideas and that is why this book is written. The ideas are those to help everybody unite and bring back the exceptionalism of this nation. It confronts directly this country's huge fiscal crises and recessions, and the devastation of the private sector which has been consuming more than it has been producing, with a mounting debt. And it gives a solid explanation of the causes of all of this, and then gives a solid basis for the correction of all of these huge problems.

Lastly, it is an adventure story that may have a happy ending. That alone may get people to read it, and in the process, they may see how they can help achieve that happy ending.

As a founder and President of the National Legal and Policy Center (NLPC), whose purpose is to promote ethics in public life, I am pleased to join in the publication of this book. While it does not necessarily represent our position on every issue, it certainly embodies the same philosophy on which NLPC was founded.

We recognize that the bigger the government, the more opportunities for corruption; and the more intervention in the economy, the more reason for special interests to seek influence. We believe that the best way to promote ethics is to reduce the size of government. And we concur with George Heideman that it is the best way to preserve our freedoms.

Let me thank Carl Horowitz of my staff for his valuable editorial assistance in the preparation of the manuscript.

Author's Introduction

Being new at the scrivener's art, I can offer no literary sophistication. I was born on an Illinois farm over 100 years ago and learned early you can lead a horse to water, but you cannot make him drink. Now I am trying to lead a bulky Washington mule (donkey?) to water, but making it drink appears to be an impossible task. But that is what I am trying to do.

This book is a primer, outlining the problems and how they can be fixed. It is a blueprint and a tool.

For over 30 years, during my active business life, I was employed by a management company that was dedicated to and also successful in developing a better tool for industry. This tool was exceptionally successful. In its applications, it multiplied production several times and in the process contributed greater precision and efficiency, helping to make many businesses profitable and saving others from failure. You might say that tool-making is my trade.

Almost 200 years ago, Sir Thomas Carlyle in his 1833 book, "Sartor Resartus", wrote: "Man is a tool-using animal. Without tools, he is nothing. With tools, he is everything."

The tools I am offering herein might not be "everything", but perhaps they can approach that in our move for the ultimates, which are Life, Liberty and the Pursuit of Happiness.

This book is a compendium of my writings over the last half-dozen years, and to that I am trying to add an evaluation following the November 6, 2012 election. I have lived for 40 percent of the existence of this nation, and with this lengthy background, I believe I am entitled to present my commentary on it.

TABLE OF CONTENTS

TABLE OF CONTENTS

PART 1

THE COMPLETE CONSTITUTION

CHAPTER ONE

THE CONSTITUTION'S MAN:
ARISTOTLE'S POLITICAL ANIMAL

*"We hold these Truths to be self-evident, that all Men
are created equal, that they are endowed by their creator
with certain unalienable Rights, that among these are
Life, Liberty, and the Pursuit of Happiness
are instituted among Men,
deriving their just Powers from the Consent of the Governed"*

The Declaration of Independence is the preamble to the Constitution, but what is the preamble to that? And who is the remarkable man those governance is addressed in the Declaration and the Constitution? Is that the same man as we have today and also going farther back the "political animal" that Aristotle called him?

These are the questions to be answered and the logical exercise I must go through before I can talk about "the complete Constitution", because by complete I mean not only its entire contents but also in time, today, as well as when written. Is there a solid consistency?

First, I deal with three attributes of man--the physical, the intellectual, and what I shall term the emotional, not only as a person but also as a "political animal."

Going back to the Greeks at the time of Aristotle, from the statues, sculpture and skeletons we can conclude that we are physically the same today as we were then. Darwin, in his "On the Origin of Species," suggested evolutionary changes in the lesser animals, but these, he emphasized, was over a much longer time span. It is an incredulous jump to assign such evolutionary changes to man.

An excellent reference for the intellectual side is William J. Bennett's, "The Book of Man: Readings on the Path to Manhood." His book argued that over the sweep of time, from Aristotle to today, that man's intellect remains the same. In discussing Aristotle's *Politics*, Bennett notes: "Long before the conception of social contract theory and democratic government, the ancient Greeks laid the foundation for Western World political thought and governance. Aristotle… was influential in developing the idea of the *poli*, or city-state, in which each man played part in deciding the "state of the community."

Bennett begins his argument that people inevitably act to obtain that which they think is good. The highest degree of good is when the political community acts. This is because man, by nature, is a "political animal." Thus, the state, even in limited form, is an inevitable outgrowth of nature.

By observing man's actions throughout history, argues Aristotle, we can deduce his innate qualities. First of all, he wants to live and to perpetuate the species. And living requires his daily sustenance, for which he must work, and he further feels that working and interacting with his fellow man makes them both more productive and is for their mutual good. But at the same time, he feels vulnerable and wants safety and security, and in this he looks for help from others, the stronger. The early tribes had their leaders to protect its member, with competing tribes constantly engaged in warfare. It dawned on them then that if they would stop fighting and merge with other tribes, the fighting would be diminished. At the same time, a leader of some sort would be needed. Thus, kings came into being. Tribal warfare was reduced, but now nation-states would wage war. Kings were only human. His subjects often were unhappy.

Aristotle concluded: "And it is a characteristic of man that he alone has any sense of good and evil, of just and unjust, and the association of living beings who have this sense makes a family and a state." The greatest benefactor of man, he argued, was he who came up with the idea for the state. But at the same time he warned that the State could be a rogue, if separated from law and justice. We can see that in the nearly 2,500 years that some things do not change. Man, in all his humanity and inhumanity, hasn't changed that much in that time.

Our 32nd president, Franklin Delano Roosevelt, in a talk about our rights said "The task of statesmanship has always been the re-definition of these rights in terms of a changing and growing social order." He may have been a clever politician but he clearly had forgotten the spirit of the Constitution he was sworn to uphold. And it had a lot to do with why his policies lengthened the Great Depression.

Bennett informs us in "The Book of Man" that the idea of men coalescing into a cohesive body was passed on from the Greeks to the Romans. But the Romans became an empire through sheer force. After the fall of Rome in the 5th century emerged the feudal monarchies of the Middle Ages. The 17th century witnessed the seeds of the Enlightenment in the form of John Locke's parliamentarism and anti-monarchism. Locke wrote "Thus that, which begins and actually constitutes any political society, is nothing but the consent of any number of freemen capable of a unit to unite."

Bennett makes clear the significance of this idea:

> *"Locke and his contemporaries believed in a return to the Aristotelian idea of self-government, that all men are equals and should be governed as equals. They believed that men were not like wolves, who roamed in packs and prayed on the weaker of their kind Instead, they viewed men more like bees where the survival of the hive is contingent on the efforts of the individuals.*
>
> *Their work sparked the fire of the American Revolution. Our Founding Fathers, for example, Alexander Hamilton, James Madison, and Thomas Jefferson, relied on the teachings of Locke, Burke, and company to give birth to the most citizen-driven, representative system of government the world has ever seen.*
>
> *For democracy to be successful, our Founding Father recognized that citizens must play their part in defending and ensuring the rights and liberties of their fellows. Samuel Adams remarked, "The liberties of our country, the freedom of our civil constitution, are worth defending against all hazards: And it is our duty to defend them against all attacks."*
>
> *Essential to the survival of the polls in ancient Greece was the belief that each man would fight for his city and*

*its well-being, whether through war, politics, or public
service The same rings true for modern democracy and
self-government "Every right implies a responsibility; every
opportunity, an obligation; every possession, a duty," said
John D. Rockefeller. Democracy is not free and our freedom
comes at the great cost and sacrifice of many heroic men
and women.*

*Because of these great citizens, the spirit of democracy
lives on in more than just constitutions, laws, and court
decisions; it is manifest in the lives of its people.*

I stand with Samuel Adams: "The liberties of our country, the freedom of our civil constitution, are worth defending against all hazards; and it is our duty to defend them against all attacks." That is why I write this book. For man in 2014 is very similar to the way he was in 1776, when the Declaration of Independence was written. The Declaration provided the rhetoric that would be codified 11 years later in the Constitution.

CHAPTER TWO

WHAT IS IN AND IS NOT IN THE CONSTITUTION

The Constitution is only the outline, the blueprint, for a system of government designed by people to govern themselves in an entirely new way. Historically, it was a continuation of and a great improvement on the English system which for centuries had been in the process of obtaining for the people a more direct part in their search for better, freer lives.

It was not a promise of Utopia. The writers knowing that man is not perfect but is always looking for perfection, so they established a flexible, dynamic system which can help man in that search, making constant changes in that direction. They set up a moral system that was fully capable of looking objectively on the present morality and in this way could give all the people practical progress in securing a better government ruling in their behalf. And that government would always be with the consent of the governed.

The Constitution provided a blueprint for civil governance. It did not make laws so much as it defined how they were to be made and enforced. It was a guide, but it did not dictate. It defined the boundaries within which laws could be enacted. And it set forth the primary duty of the federal government: providing physical protection for its citizens.

The Constitution had a clear precedent in the English system, which had been in use by the 13 colonies. And it was superbly balanced. Governance was to be separated into three distinct functions: legislative, executive and judicial. And its allocation of authority exercised by the sovereign, was assigned to the federal government, state governments, and the ultimate sovereign, the people.

Unfortunately, over the last several decades we have been in the process of dismantling this legal infrastructure. A series of presidencies, exceeding the boundaries of its lawful constitutional authority, has been eroding powers properly delegated to Congress. And even the Supreme Court has become politicized. Routinely, the federal government overrides state authority to accomplish supposedly national goals.

There is some flexibility to promote cooperation. An example of this is in the passage of laws the president may veto a law passed by Congress, but the Congress can override that veto. In at least one instance, there has been tainting and corruption caused by overriding of the integrity of the sovereignty of the three parts. This takes place every ten years in the process of redistricting Congressional districts because the Constitution never provides for Congressional districts with their own sovereignty. The representation of the state is set by two senators for each state; that is fixed. The representation for the people of each state is set for the country but varies by state in proportion to population per the census every ten years.

But under the present system, it is not the people but the legislature of each state that sets these sub-areas of sovereignty, usually in a very disorderly and combative way, with the judiciary frequently called in to help. The serious faults and harmful effects of this are widely known and there is much complaint, as there should be. But it would be very simple to correct all of this and abide by the Constitution if a fixed formula was adopted, as the document calls for. Later in this book I outlined that system of state-wide election of representatives, thereby representing the interests of all of the people of the state in the House.

At various times and from various sources there has been much thinking that perhaps this extreme rigidity should be altered by at least allowing some competitive interplay among the parts. In a quite thorough investigation of this proposition, Michael S. Greve, in his recent book "The Upside-Down Constitution," has discussed this. I certainly agree with his title, and most of the well-supported contents but he would appear to have some tolerance for this flexibility principally in the areas of the sovereignty of the federal and state governments, but I am suspicious that in this tolerance he has vanquished the major objective of the Constitution, which is the dominant sovereignty of the people.

CHAPTER THREE

THE UNWRITTEN PART: ITS MANY VIOLATIONS.

In the foregoing as a student of the Constitution I have attempted to show an appreciation and understanding of what an exceptional document it is. I have alluded to the fact that there are some unwritten and powerful provisions that are just as important, in fact perhaps more important, than the written words that had been added as part of the Bill of Rights in 1791. This chapter expands and elaborates on many of these enumerated parts.

Among these other rights that might have been referred to were the bodies of civil and criminal laws (and English common law) that were accepted as law by the colonies. There were also two other rights that might have been included but evidently were not because it was thought as being accepted and not needed. These are (1) the right of parents to educate their children as they see fit, and (2) the right of everyone to control and contract for his human services, his labor, as he saw fit.

It should be noted that education in the colonies was an entirely private matter; there were no public schools. In no place does the Constitution ever mention education. Likewise in the colonies each citizen had the right to control his own labor.

There are two other things in the Constitution partially hidden which bear directly on these human rights and that they be freely exercised as long as they complied with the civil and criminal laws passed by the people. These are (1) habeas corpus, dating a long way back in English history. Article I, Section 9, Clause 2 says: "The Privilege of the Writ of Habeas Corpus shall not be suspended, unless when in Cases of Rebellion or Invasion the public safety may require it." And (2) "No Bill of Attainder... shall be passed." Article I, Section 9, Clause 3.

The Heritage Guide to the Constitution, page 153, says:

> *From the time of the Civil War, the Supreme Court continuously expanded the availability of habeas relief. Under the common-law tradition, habeas relief obtained only when the court (or the sheriff or warden) could not show jurisdiction over the prisoner. Federal courts, however, expanded habeas relief to include a broader definition of "custody" than mere arrest, including most defects found at trial. In Brown v. Allen, the Supreme Court dispensed with earlier limitations and accorded habeas relief to any person held in violation of the Constitution.*

Today, based on a pronouncement by Justice Rehnquist, habeas corpus is a right of equitable relief that courts have the power to contract or expand as is needed, in both State and Federal courts.

The prohibition against bills of attainder continues as strong as ever. James Madison in Federalist No. 14 said "Bills of attainder.. and laws impairing the obligation of contracts are contrary to the first principles of the social compact, and to every principle of sound legislation." The Framers forbade bills of attainder as part of the strategy to do away with the most serious historical instances of legislative tyranny by state or national legislatures, and the Supreme Court has insisted that such bills may affect the life of an individual, or may confiscate his property, or may do both.

The meaning of habeas corpus has now been extended much beyond the assertion by the subjects that "they have a body," to become a beacon for human freedom.

Nothing is more private than our sexual lives but in the proposed health coverage this completely disappears. The government is telling us to forget totally about our personal responsibility; if something bad happens, "not to worry, you are insured." This covers unexpected pregnancies, an event that is not insurable because of "adverse selection" and the moral problem. Also all preventive "contraception" and similar procedures are covered. Pregnancy is not a disease; only abnormal conditions arising with it are treated as a sickness. Abortion cannot be covered as an insurable risk also because of adverse election plus the moral part of it. In essence, it is assisted suicide which is not legal in any of our states.

Regular, routine preventive actions in health care are, of course, very good but there are no good reasons why they should be covered by insurance (if they could be), as in almost all cases they are well within the means of the individual to cover; they are similar to "deductibles" in property insurance. Everybody has a legitimate lifetime need for health care. What do we have right now? Nobody knows but everyone fears. We have almost 3,000 pages of rambling rhetoric and regulations incomprehensible and incomplete details, and complete confusion. In a democracy, we should have simple laws that the people can comprehend and understand, but here we have tautological tyranny. What is called insurance is not true insurance. And the law seeks to do the impossible in trying to define the bounds of physical well-being at public expense.

As a final note, what is insidious about all of this is the fact that most of this tyranny is being imposed by a new class of rulers that have crept into power-- radical rulers with radical agenda-- the regulatory bureaucracy of unelected officials now holding the reigns of power. Our votes and our Constitution no longer count.

Today, these "entitlements" have been completely inflated beyond meeting economic needs but to provide almost everything else they may want, not only in health care and retirement income but in our private lives. The answer is to get back to basics within the framework of our Constitution.

What is health? Health is a personal condition meaning a state of being hale and sound in body and mind, being free from physical disease or pain. The government in its concern over the financial aspect of this broad subject has overstepped its bounds. Insurance has been a sound, private institution for centuries, in which people facing potentially calamitous risks have transferred and contracted that risk to insurers who have the resources to handle them in return for periodic payments known as premiums. Government "insurance," however, is nothing like this. It would charge premiums that are not actuarially sound and then it would not retain them as reserve funds to pay claims. It is a pay-as-you-go process, including increased benefits without increased premiums, in an economy afloat on persistent inflation. This "insurance" amounts to a fraud.

The first entitlement, Social Security, was started in 1935 as intergenerational insurance program. The federal government effectively would do the "saving for a day" for people who presumably were unable to do it themselves. The government would compel employers and employees alike to make contributions in the form of payroll taxes. Congress at that time actually discussed how to invest these funds, but could not agree on how to do it.

CHAPTER FOUR

POWER VERSUS PRINCIPLES

The following contains some further thoughts on the state of man's humanity. What prompts me to add this is that in history we should not forget Athens versus Troy, and in my personal history I should not forget the bloody nose I received at a Sunday school picnic in my youth. Combativeness, of course, is part of man's nature – his survival instinct. And with that comes the aftermath – the joy of victory or the sadness of defeat. Everybody has a passion to experience the former.

Because of this, there is an evitable battle between power and principles. Our Founders clearly recognized this but in their idealism they may have been too optimistic. They depended too much on demos. They felt and hoped that when power threatened to prevail, the good common sense of the people (James Madison termed it "the cool deliberations of the community") would prevail at the polls and correct the course. But this also unwisely presumed a very clear-thinking populace that would clearly see the correct principles.

Here is the real source of the present impasse, with the two dominant political parties engaged in gridlock, representing little but power against power. It is true that they talk about "issues" but issues are too often merely reflections of their self-interests that only a dominance of power can satisfy. Rarely in these debates do we hear reference to the Constitution and man's solidly-based rights that are deep within it.

Each party feels that it must rule, wanting almost absolute power, and in this they approximate the historical kings who claimed "divine rights" which could not be questioned even when actions frequently were more devilish than divine. But our principles have been soundly developed by men reasoning among themselves in a democratic process, and are the products of men with inalienable rights conferred by their Creator. Further they acknowledge that in their search for perfection they might have flaws, and the structure of this unique form of government lets them admit their mistakes and try over.

The negative economic effects of this battle royal are huge but too often are not recognized or correctly priced. The exercise of power today requires much money to support it and the powers look to taxes on the people to support them. In this process the provisions and limitations of the law and the strict rules of the Constitution itself are almost completely forgotten. Money here further sublimates principles and gives dominance to power. In this chaos, nobody gives any thoughts about what the proper governing principles are and the fact that they must be consistent with the limited powers our government is supposed to have.

Aristotle astutely asserted, as previously noted, that man can have too much freedom and, denying law and order, can create injustices, using his intellect and the same freedom. This ironical situation he termed "the worst."

As covered in a later chapter (The Poison of Excessive Partisanship and its Constitutional Antidote"), James Madison was correct when he observed "No free country has even been without parties which are a natural offspring of freedom", yet today some people still maintain that the Constitution governs parties. The realities, however, show that that is not the case with very harmful effects resulting.

For 150 years most American believed that the Constitution guided us on a straight and proper path on which the private sector could freely maximize production, and that the government would be limited in its powers. But this has changed very much after the Progressives came to power. Under this philosophy, government would take an aggressive role in promoting progress and prosperity. There always has been opposition to this, but the costs of this wrongheaded philosophy, tangible and intangible, have become more evident than ever.

This book is written in an effort to awaken this country from where we have gone wrong, analyzing it from the standpoint of sound economics, and pointing how we can correct course. Having faith in this country and the soundness of the principles upon which it was founded, the author firmly believes it can be done but notes realistically that will take a long time. At stake is not only the future of this country, but also Western civilization.

CHAPTER FIVE

APPLE TREES AND CHERRY TREES
(THE PARABLE OF THE FREE MARKETERS
AND THE SOCIALISTS)

Once upon a time there were some people who were free-market capitalists ever since they were placed on this earth by the Creator. They planted apple trees, fertilized them, and then feasted on the fruit when it was ripe, saying how lucky they were that they would have more apples to feast on next year.

But then some of these people, in their blindness, drifted away. They did not plant apple trees but instead found a cherry tree. In their hunger to get at the cherries, they cut down the tree. After feasting on the cherries, they reflected how good they were and assured each other that they would find more cherry trees next year. But in the next year they could not find any cherry trees and complained to their leaders: "Why did you cut down that cherry tree last year?" But the leaders lied. They denied they had cut down the cherry trees, saying it was the free marketers who had done it. Go ask them for some of their fruit.

The free marketers gave them some of their apples, apple stones and cherry stones to plant. The "blind" quickly ate the fruit but returned the stones, saying "These are pits! Next year we will expect you to give us some more fruit."

Thus endeth the parable. The lesson: Supporters of the free market are right to ask: 'Who are you to say I cannot do with what is my own? Methinks you have an evil eye.'

CHAPTER SIX

CONGRESS HAS NO RIGHT TO GIVE AWAY THE PEOPLE'S MONEY

David Crockett

In a section of William Bennett's "The Book of Man" called "Not Yours to Give", the author recounts the stalwart defense of the real Constitution given by Davie Crockett, hero of the Battle of the Alamo. Crockett (1786-1836) was an authentic American folk hero, and in the 1830s represented his Tennessee district in the U.S. House of Representatives. Of Crockett's tract, "Not Yours to Give," Bennett says: "Here is a great example of civic manhood. It is redolent of contemporary debate about the purpose and responsibility of government and efforts to restrain the expansion of the federal government."

In response to a bill appropriating money for the benefit of a widow of a distinguished naval officer, which was well supported, Crockett strongly objected, saying "We have the right as individuals to give away as much of our own money as we please in charity, but as member of Congress we have no right to appropriate a dollar of the public money." It was defeated. Later, when Crockett was asked why he opposed it, he explained that several years previously he had approved a charity donation for victims of an extensive house fire in Washington, but subsequently, as he was campaigning, he talked to a man plowing his field who knew him and also knew that he had voted for the house-fire welfare bill. The plowman said because of that he would never vote for Crockett. The plowman said because the Constitution to be worth anything must be held sacred, and rigidly observed in all of its provisions… Congress has no right to give charity; individual members may give as much of their own money as they please but they have no right to touch a dollar of the public money for that purpose."

I stand with Davie Crockett and that plowman (perhaps because once I was a plowman myself.) Our Congress now gives giving several trillion dollars each year, and there is no Crockett to complain. Social Security was started as a modest insurance program, but grown into a behemoth. And the new health care law may wind up dwarfing even that.

CHAPTER SEVEN

WASHINGTON'S FAREWELL ADDRESS

George Washington's fatherly advice contained his farewell address of September 17, 1797 still applies today. It is well that we heed his words. For our first president over 200 years ago foresaw how an overambitious government can corrupt the nation. After extolling the pride of patriotism in this young and vibrant nation, Mr. Washington warned of changes which might endanger the nation.

Washington at length expressed eloquently the dangers of excessive partisanship, parties and factions. He said they were destructive and fatal tendencies to be avoided, subverting the power of the people as the selfish parties seek selfish power. He admitted that parties possibly in a free country are useful, but they are not to be encouraged.

He stressed the importance of national defense.

He warned about credit and the accumulation of debt, a burden which would be imposed on posterity.

He said the power to tax is the power to enslave the people,

He pointed out to have "political Prosperity", religion and morality is indispensable.

He warned that in administration one department should not encroach upon another, resulting in despotism. He stressed the checks and balances that are in the Constitution.

The purpose of this book is to show that Washington's forebodings have come to full fruition, and that we should take action to correct our course.

PART 2

AN INCOMPLETE AMERICA

INTRODUCTION

Materialism may be a way of saying "the economy," but our pride as a nation comes from things much deeper. To understand this, we must understand what wealth really is and how it is produced. It is not static, it is a living stream, and we should overlook the frequent pools and puddles that take place when at times it is dammed or obstructed. Further, what makes a healthy, moving stream are the forces necessary to produce it, with dependable sources and accommodating outlets. We must look to the production of the stream of wealth and what happens to it, its consumption. A recession is a slowing down in the stream of wealth; a depression is when obstructions in the stream dry the water up.

The complete man is more than a materialist. To achieve contentment, he must learn to live with his fellow man. Government is necessary, but it cannot produce the values that make one content and able to cooperate.

CHAPTER EIGHT

THOMAS JEFFERSON; THE COMPLETE AMERICAN

Socialism, in theory and practice, is the antithesis of constitutional principle. The following is an indictment. And the primary vehicle is Thomas Jefferson. Jon Meacham's 2012 book, "Thomas Jefferson. The Art of Power," makes a strong case for Jefferson as a major inspiration for resisting socialism.

Thomas Jefferson in the exactly 50 years from his completing the Declaration of Independence on July 4, 1776 to his death on July 4, 1826, was arguably this country's most eminent statesman. It would be hard to imagine anyone since then who has matched him. He had an excellent education and was fascinated by the Enlightenment philosophers. Jefferson, first and foremost, sought to apply the lessons of the Enlightenment to civil governance. In the process, he widened our national life in all respects.

In the opening of the Declaration of Independence he identified the character of the enlightened man. And in the next fifty years he constantly reminded his countrymen of this enlightenment and its promise. Throughout, he exercised great powers but he never or one moment let that power compromise those principles. He kept reminding the people that this was a nation where people governed and not one where the people are governed.

All .of our most prominent presidents since 1826, and from all parties, have (at least in their more lucid moments) remembered Thomas Jefferson and his message. Abraham Lincoln did as much in 1859, two years before he became president, writing: "The principles of Jefferson are the definitions and axioms of a free society. Those who deny freedom to others, deserve it not for themselves; and, under a just God, cannot long retain it."

Theodore Roosevelt rode rough-shod in Jefferson's shadow, even to the extent of becoming an independent, running against Woodrow Wilson in 1912, and this unfortunately resulted in the election of Wilson.

In 1932, in Minnesota, Franklin Delano Roosevelt sought the mantle of Jefferson, saying, "It was the purpose of Jefferson to teach the country that the solidarity Federalism is only a partial one, and to build a great Nation the interests of all groups in every part must be considered." Of course, as has been proven many times, security cannot be found solely on national unity, it takes much more than that, including a perceptive minority.

In 1948, Harry S. Truman invoked Jefferson when he said: "I have a profound faith in the people of this country. I believe in their commonsense. They love freedom and that love for freedom and justice is not dead. Our people believe today, as Jefferson did, that men were not born with saddles on their backs to be ridden by the privileged few."

In December 1988, Ronald Reagan speaking at Jefferson's beloved University of Virginia (which he had founded) spoke at length about Jefferson, showing a complete understanding of him. He noted that Jefferson well knew from personal experience how disorderly the world can be but that he also believed "that man had received from God a precious gift of enlightenment--the gift of reason, a gift that could extract from the chaos of life, meaning, truth, order."

How can we put together all of these present difference between the free market, limited-government people and those devoted to unlimited government, market-control people? This has gone far beyond Federalism. I shall not quibble; I shall correctly refer to the latter as "Socialists."

In 1913, the year Congress established the income tax and the Federal Reserve System, we lay the groundwork for socialism. This represented an overreach of the proper scope of government, extending it to control over the economy. But in an objective evaluation of Socialism, I am willing to forget the Constitution as originally written, and look at history, of which Jefferson is an indisputable part. Jefferson called upon all of the people to exercise "the standard of reason." (Truman referred to this as "commonsense."). He called upon the inner man (as we should today) to reason together with his fellow man. In so doing, our nation can reach common agreement on the issues. To understand as much is to realize that Socialism does not work as a system of thought.

In every nation socialism has been put in place, the result has been failure and often great tragedy. Even in milder form, as in the European Union, the results have been wanting. And here in the United States, we are facing a potential disaster because of misguided laws, policies and court decisions out in placer that have served to dramatically increase the level of intervention by government in the economy. Our debts continue to grow to the point of being unsustainable.

So much for history--it proves Socialism does not work as a system but is an utter failure. Now, being charitable, let us look to see if there is any solid philosophy that can support it. Why did the Progressivists want a bigger government (and more money) and how did they justify it? They showed understandable compassion when they noted that amidst patches of prosperity there were large patches of poverty. Not knowing how to fix that within the free-market system, they jumped to the conclusion that the government should take over. They perceived the practitioners in the free market to be selfish and greedy, and the free-market system needed government help to correct this. It was a social condition that needed help.

They were blind to "the unseen hand" of Adam Smith. In that system with each person following his own best interests the result is the best interests of all are served. Clearly, they did not understand the Constitutional system.

Our Founders started out with the sole purpose of designing a structure of government where the people would remain in control of it as much as possible, and they addressed only that portion of the total environment that is government, overlooking that part of it which is how people make their living and the total culture that surrounds that. It was not to be a codification of laws; it assigned functions to the branches of government but did not include any laws, per se. The Supreme Court was to adjudicate the laws, whatever they might be. But as certain colonies would not ratify without some assurance on some legal matters, a Bill of Rights was adopted which opened a Pandora's box. That brought into play what is really the preamble to Constitution: the Declaration of Independence.

There is another negative about Socialism when comparing it with the free-enterprise system mandated for us, and that is in the dictatorial, the king-can-do-no-wrong system of Socialism, it is difficult to correct even the most obvious mistakes of government, whereas the system designed for us readily assumed that man is not perfect but also that he is constantly searching for perfection. Accordingly, the system as designed calls for this constant search for perfection.

As stated, that which started out to be merely an agreement on a structure of government emerged as what really can be called a miracle. In defining the rights of man brought forth by the Declaration, that enlightened philosophy also became entrenched in a government structure calling for enforcement of those rights.

Jefferson was in bitter conflict always with Hamilton and the other Federalists who believed in a strong central government. He here was a strong advocate of a people's government, including the absolute rights of the minority. He was not about to compromise them. He called for government and church to recognize the rights of the other. There was to be no trespass. The government was to govern but in the process it could do nothing to deprive the people of the right to peaceably worship. But as it is a government of the people, it need not and cannot operate in a void but can properly reflect the culture of the people it governs.

Hamilton and the other Federalists fought hard for a very strong central government, and here Jefferson continued his firm opposition to that, not only representing the rights of minorities but also the rights of all in religion. President Obama, who has never shown any signs of having read or understood Thomas Jefferson, has set forth a consummate and super-Federalism stand on all of this. In his stand for social considerations to prevail, he has swept all of this, including religion, under the rug.

Today, this country has forsaken Jefferson, not to mention Supreme Court Chief Justice John Marshall, who, in an outstanding decision in *McCulloch v. Maryland* (1819), ruled that the federal government should not usurp the authority of state governments.

CHAPTER NINE

WHAT IS WEALTH?

*The principles of wealth-creation transcend time, people,
and place. Governments which deliberately subvert them
by denouncing God, smothering faith, destroying freedom,
and confiscating wealth have impoverished their people.
Communism works only in Heaven, where they don't need it,
and in Hell, where they've already got it.*
~President Ronald Reagan~

As a nation and as culture we appear to have quite strong and stubborn insistence for precision in things physical but unfortunately this is not extended to many things metaphysical. From this, we may be suffering more than we know for the lack of it. This is particularly true in the field of economics.

With this in mind, and recognizing a personal guilt here, I made time to take a basic, inward look to detect perhaps my lack of understanding of the actions people take in trying to make a living. And so I went to Webster's Collegiate Dictionary.

*"Economics: The science that investigates the conditions and
laws affecting the production, distribution and consumption
of wealth or the human means of satisfying human desires."*

And Wealth, simply: *"The abundant possession of resources."*

What people call "wealth" is really the evidence of wealth which they see and perceive, and in this perception there are various kinds, incorporating degrees of "goodness." Historically the ability of our special economic system to produce wealth is the area of our greatest pride; it is that which is the real basis for the ultimate, Life, Liberty and the Pursuit of Happiness.

Here, also, there are many misconceptions, and misconceptions in material things are frequently characterized as "fool's gold", alluding of course to a special kind of value given to gold, the metal. If we are given a gold brick to hold, it may momentarily give us the glow and the aura of wealth but it adds nothing to our personal wealth.

Wealth is not static; it is a moving thing. It can be likened to a steady stream of tiny drops of water moving to satisfy our desires. It is the recognition of such tiny particles that constitutes wealth. They do not rest.

Wealth is the product of people working together, and the more smoothly and in a balanced fashion they do this, the more wealth they accumulate. From that we may conclude that the free market, viewed objectively, is the only system that works. Adam Smith (1776) wrote "The Wealth of Nations" rather than "The Wealth of People," but he was anything but a forerunner of the progressives. He considered people as intelligent enough to make their own decisions. What is more, he maintained that it is "the unseen hand" of all people reasoning and working together to meet their personal needs that results in the greatest wealth production for not only them but also for their nation.

As stated, economics is all about wealth, and to understand economics we must first understand what wealth is and how it is created. Most wealth has physical aspects but it is basically and mostly a concept in the mind. To understand it, it would be beneficial to review the late journalist Warren Brookes' 1982 book, "The Economy in Mind."

Brookes regarded economics as a metaphysical rather than a mathematical science. For him, intangible spiritual values are at least as important as physical assets. Describing that wealth is principally the result of imagination, innovation, and individual creativity, each of which are unlimited. He argues eloquently that the decline in U.S. strength during the Seventies had more to do with a decline in goodness than from specific policies or leaders.

The mistake made by most monetary economists is that they think that economics is all about "money". Overlooking the fact that the true value of money is its mechanical part; it is the essential part it plays in its orderly exchange in the market place. Yes, money is not wealth but it is its rapid stream (the velocity of the turnover of money) that is more important than the volume of money held by the people. This misconception is frequently held by the public but surprisingly and too often held by some of those who allege to be economists.

It is frequently said and accepted that happiness is more valuable than money. But it is the flow of money in the process that brings happiness and the satisfaction of our desires.

George Gilder who wrote the forward to "The Economy in Mind," had an article in *National Review* of August 13, 2012, "Unleash the Mind" which begins:

> America's wealth is not an inventory of goods; it is
> an organic entity, a fragile pulsing fabric of ideas,

expectations, loyalties, moral commitments, visions. To vivisect it for redistribution is to kill it. As President Mitterrand's French technocrat discovered in the 1980s, and President Obama's quixotic ecocrats are discovering today, government managers of complex systems of wealth soon find they are administering an industrial corpse, a socialized Solyndra. All riches must finally fall into the gap between thought and things. Governed by mind but caught in matter, assets must afford an income stream that is expected to continue. The expectation may shift as swiftly as thought, but things, alas, are all too solid and slow to change. The kaleidoscope of shifting valuations, flashing gains and losses as it turned in the hands of time, in the grip of "news," distributes and redistributes the wealth of the world far more quickly and surely than any scheme of the state.

Gilder concluded:

The key issue in economics is not aligning incentives with some putative public good but aligning power with knowledge. Business investments bring both a financial and an epistemic yield Capitalism catalytically joins the two. Capitalist economies grow because they award wealth to its creators, who have already proven that they can increase it. Their proof was always the service of others rather than themselves. As Peter Drucker has written, within companies there are no profit centers, only cost centers. Whether a particular cost yields a profit is determined voluntarily by customers and investors.

> Capitalism feeds on information that is outside of
> the company itself and therefore under the control
> of others. Only an altruistic orientation can tap the
> outside incandescence of information and learning
> that determine the success of capitalism's gifts.

Wealth-building this country must be in substantial balance. For our first 150 years, this country operated and prospered with a substantially-balanced economy, with the supply-side process spurring the exceptional progress. There was balance in government generally, doing those things required to support the free-market structure and little more. Under such conditions the private sector also experienced a generally-balanced existence. It produced not only enough for its own needs but also sold and exported abroad many of our products and services. And the less affluent knew there was always a great opportunity for them to advance. For the poor and needy, society provided a compassionate safety net.

This out-of-balance condition did not result from this country running out of resources. We have always been and continue to be very rich in resources. But there have been many false alarms about that. Now, adding to that there have been irrational demands that we do not even use those that we have. Some in our government have joined the UN and foreign governments in a global warming hoax. To fight this, The Committee For A Constructive Tomorrow issued a special report in July 2012, which stated: "Twenty years ago, the 1992 UN Earth Summit in Rio de Janeiro was the environmental movement's Woodstock, the kickoff of a massive world wide campaign that led to the "global warming" scare and the Kyoto Protocol, the ongoing regulatory onslaught, and the Agenda 21 blueprint for worldwide Green governance. Rio also paved the way for Al Gore and other "Save the Earth" gurus to fatten their pocketbooks with highly subsidized ventures which promised much but delivered little environmental goods."

We certainly have not had a shortage of labor. For several centuries people have been streaming into this country, and that continues.

Our most damaging shortage is that we have not had able and intelligent statesmen who know how to govern. This is in spite of our exceptional Constitution outlining clearly how we people can join together to govern ourselves and in the process attain a quality of life and prosperity never before seen in history.

During the last half of the 19th century when certain problems and excesses arose which inept leadership failed to handle, some were too quick to blame "the system." They concluded that a better system would require those elected to hire experts who could operate more efficiently. These" Progressives" came into power during 1900-15. An objective review of what has happened since, here and in other countries, reveals this to have been a lamentable development. No enclave of experts, and particularly where they are impressed with their own power, can work as efficiently as free enterprise. Further, one of the admirable features of our kind of government is that experimentation is permitted, and when one policy proves defective and imperfect, we readily resume the search for perfection. No power-dominated, dictatorial government can do that.

Perhaps our major mistake is that in the government of people we are betting on mere hypotheses and ideologies. In the 17th century John Locke gave us a set of propositions, and from this our Founders gave us a system of governance, with no guarantee of success. Thus we should not be too disappointed that glitches have developed. We should bravely start over and correct the glitches.

Changes in humanity and our culture, including our feelings and ways of thinking, always have been behind the thinking of the more enlightened.

First of all, this requires vast changes in government and re-duced size. The thinking of the people must be changed and they must be convinced our present depressed economy is the fault of the government as it has taken too much away from the people; this is becoming a socialistic state and the hardships that causes can easily be seen in Europe today. This is a huge problem and perhaps the best we can hope for now are some emergency mea-sures and compromises, and be patient with big government until we can gradually change its size.

What can and must be done.

To get an understanding of the seriousness of our deeply-im-bedded problems we must go back at least 50 years, and I know of no other or better source, succinctly summarized, than that given by Brookes. Extracts from it are footnoted to this chap-ter. But a similar deep analysis of what has happened in the last dozen years is required before we can even begin to turn things around and keep us from falling off the cliff over which we dan-gle in 2012.

During mid-century, bad economics and court decisions accel-erated an alarming set of trends. As per the footnote, Keynes got this started when he proposed that the government could smooth out the business cycle simply by more clever management of the aggregate demand, pumping it up during periods of recession and tightening down during periods of boom, and the combination of government spending and money-supply control as the basic tools in the process.

Unfortunately, the politicians concluded that if a little such government interference in the private sector was good, more would be much better. This was grabbed as a quick fix, with Nixon lamenting, "We're all Keynesians now." Under President Reagan there was some attempt to counter this, but in the 90s it started all over again but much greater in magnitude with a stock market bubble followed by the catastrophe of 2008-09.

The quantitative data quoted by Brookes for this early period are truly shocking, but if similar analyses are made for the current period, they would seem modest! Brookes pointed out the following, among other supporting data:

"Throughout the 1960s (the decade of our latest and least inflationary growth), the supply side of our economy got 50%-60% of all credit while the demand side got only 40%-45%, and the government took only 9%-12%. But in the 1970s, the demand side took over, with 60%-65% of all credit going not to productivity (plant and equipment) but to stimulating consumer demand, with government taking 25% of all credit dollars."

Further, "during the period 1970-1978, the total credit market in the United States expanded 263%--more than twice the total GNP growth of 114% and seven times as fast as the real growth in goods and services of only 15%. More important, the demand-side credit grew nearly three times as fast as the supply-side credit, with consumer credit growing 486% in just eight years, when even inflated consumer purchases grew only 117%. In other words, consumer credit grew four times as fast as total consumer purchases and 11 times as fast as real good output, as the nation moved to a credit-card economy, tremendously expanding demand beyond real supply."

But it can readily be accepted that these out-of-balance relationships of those time multiplied greatly during the last dozen years. And our own excesses were also exported abroad, with many of the derivatives from sub-prime mortgages being sold abroad, increasing our own supply of credit and money.

We need a revolution, not just correction, in our thinking and this must be from top to bottom. Many "mechanical" things can be done, such as reforming the Internal Revenue Code to reduce its emphasis on promoting consumption, to reforming the massive entitlements to make them more sustainable, to drastically cutting all the over-sized expansions of government operations that have taken place. Basically, of course, it requires a massive change in our thinking, in our basic philosophy; we must embrace free-market capitalism, which makes possible economic growth. Only with such restoration will we be able to depart from the precipice over which we now precariously hang.

What is not recognized is the devastating role of the two chief entitlements now in place, Social Security and Medicare, in robbing America of capital. Without privatization and radical reform in these programs, this process cannot be reversed. The Federal Insurance Contribution Act of 1935 now requires employees and employers to divert all of the wealth produced by most businesses and industries during five of the working days each week to the government, and the government has failed in its duty to fund these contributions but has spent it on its enlarged operations, including therein much stifling regulations which further reduce production. Under these depressing conditions, there can never be balance, and we will continue to lose wealth at an accelerating rate.

The ugly head of monopoly also adds to this devastation. For wealth to be produced in a free enterprise economy there must be fair, free and active competition throughout. Although we give it lip service, we tolerate and promote big business and big government sponsoring, constructing and operating huge monopolies which not only have a dysfunctional effect on the general economy but promote special interests that are also huge negatives. And then when they become too big to fail, the government asks the taxpayers to bail them out, thus taking further resources from the people who have already suffered, deprived of any opportunity to create wealth. When pro-active, real competition is restores throughout economy, no business will become too big to fail, and all businesses would be aided to become big enough to succeed. This can be only if and when the heavy and fat fist of government is taken off of this nation's economic scales.

As a final and full indictment of big government, it should be noted that it has even moved into the private area of business in the accounting for wealth. Man in attempting to record his wealth uses the art of accountancy, trying to capture and set down the stream of transactions that constitute and are the evidence of the units of wealth being experienced in producing, distributing and consuming the goods and services that are desired. Beginning in the 15th century in Italy where the system of double-entry bookkeeping was devised, accountants acting as the handmaiden of the lawyers have in the accounts recognized the ownership of assets and the owing of liabilities. There has always existed between these two an unwritten contract that this would be done correctly in the best interest of both, and they have developed through the years generally-accepted accounting principles and similar disciplines. But even here the government has moved in, denied that contractual relationship (unconstitutionally!), passing Sarbanes-Oxley and other laws. The results have been very bad, with the financial statements becoming so long and detailed that they have lost their usefulness. These heavy-handed acts of the government which have deprived the users of financial statements of the professionalism and material presentations urgently needed.

The Failure of Keynesianism

It was John Maynard Keynes who in 1936 lifted money out of its natural role as a medium of exchange or barter and gave it a new economic and political significance by calling it "aggregate demand" and by theorizing that the major reason for boom-and-bust business cycles was the unevenness of aggregate demand, and the failure of this demand to keep the economy moving, particularly during recessions. He proposed that the government could smooth out the business cycle simply by more clever management of the aggregate demand (alias money supply), pumping it up during periods of recession and tightening down during periods of boom, using the combination of government spending and money-supply control as the basic tools in the process.

Unfortunately, the politicians heard only the first part of Keynes's proposition—the part that called for stimulating the economy by monetary and fiscal expansion, and it wasn't long before this one-sided and simplistic pursuit of Keynesianism produced rapidly rising inflation and rapidly deteriorating investment. In the process, the entire complexion of the U.S. economy has been altered. Prior to 1965, our average real annual growth rate was 3.5% and our average inflation rate was 1.9%—while our money supply grew less than 3.5% per year. Since 1966, however, our average real growth rate has fallen to 2.5%, and our average inflation rate is now more than 8%. GNP growth has dropped by 30%

and inflation has more than quadrupled, while money growth has surged to 8% or more.

Fifteen years of stimulating consumer demand in this fashion painted our economy into a very tight corner, with the result that in 1980 and again in 1981 we had to witness the tragic process of throwing over 3 million men and women out of work solely to attempt to restore both the Federal Reserve's and the dollar's credibility. After churning money out like a gusher (right through Carter's failed reelection bid in November 1980), the Federal Reserve finally slammed the gates for good in the spring of 1981.

In this way, 3 million Americans who had been put back to work by the highly stimulative monetary policies of 1977-79 under President Carter suddenly found themselves being sacrificed to fight the double-digit inflation which these deliberately inflationary policies had produced, as the economy was once again dragged through the wringer for the sake of saving the value of an otherwise worthless paper dollar.

The Credit Explosion

One driving force behind this rapid money-supply growth has been an exploding level of demand-side credit, fueled in large measure by deliberate government policies and by an accommodating attitude at the Federal Reserve. The idea behind these policies was that one could get much more "bang for the buck" by expanding consumer demand through government deficits and federally assisted borrowing than by the slower process of waiting for (or encouraging) private capital investment in productivity (supply). Their effect can be seen in Table 4-8 which shows just how drastically the nation's basic credit markets shifted from supporting supply (corporate and farm investment) to promoting consumer demand (consumer and government credit).

Throughout the 1960s (the decade of our best, and least-inflationary, growth), the supply side of our economy got 55%-60% of all the credit, while the demand side got only 40%-45%, and government took only 9%-12%. But in the 1970s the demand side took over, with 60%-65% of all credit going, not to productivity (plant and equipment), but to stimulating consumer demand, with government taking 2.5% of all credit dollars.

During the period 1970-78, the total credit market in the United States expanded by 263%—more than twice the total GNP growth of 114% and seven times as fast as the real growth in goods and services of only 35%. More important, the demand-side credit grew nearly three times as fast as the supply-side credit, with consumer credit growing 486% in just eight years, when even inflated consumer purchases grew only 117%. In other words, consumer credit grew four times as fast as total consumer purchases and 11 times as fast as real goods output, as the nation moved to a credit-card economy, tremendously expanding demand beyond real supply.

What the public does not realize is the degree to which the explosion in consumer borrowing was directly assisted by federal programs (housing, education loans, etc.). In addition to the more than $400 billion in direct new federal debt issued to the public in 1969-81 to cover deficits, the federal government also added more than $290 billion in federally assisted or guaranteed credit to the consumer markets, mostly in housing. In 1978 alone, for example, $51 billion of the $145.9 billion in new consumer credit was directly sponsored by the federal government, in addition to the more than $59 billion borrowed directly by the U.S. Treasury to cover budget deficits.

It is this explosion in demand-side credit (accommodated by the Federal Reserve in money growth) that has fueled the U.S. economy's unprecedented combination of declining productivity (weakening supply) and double-digit inflation (accelerating demand).

At the very time when rapidly rising marginal tax rates were choking private investment, savings, and real economic growth, the U.S. credit markets were also under heavy siege by the federal Treasury. At the very time when interest rates should have been coming down to allow for investment in recovery, the U.S. economy faced a credit crunch. While part of that credit crunch resulted from the Federal Reserve's somewhat "yo-yo" efforts to get the raging money supply under control, a significant share of it stemmed from the mounting federal demands on U.S. credit markets.

As OMB Director-to-be David Stockman warned with prescience in December 1980, "President Reagan will inherit thoroughly disordered credit and capital markets, punishingly high interest rates, and a hair-trigger market psychology poised to respond strongly to early economic policy signals in either favorable or unfavorable ways." What worried Stockman was the degree to which much of the federal borrowing had nothing to do with the federal budget hut consisted of off-budget items in the form of loan guarantees and federally-sponsored credit, mostly through the Federal Financing Bank.

CHAPTER TEN

A COUNTRY OUT OF BALANCE
EQUILIBRIUM WILL BRING EQUALITY

"Give us this day our daily bread!" No matter what the country or the religion, this is the prayer of the people. But nobody can eat bread until it is produced. Production must come before consumption. But this country has completely forgotten this. Supply-side economics understands that the resources that result from the supply process go back into the economy to initiate further production, but today when that smooth flow has been completely interrupted by government that insists on doing much more than it should, then the process is grounded, and the balance is upset.

For our first 150 years, this country operated and prospered with a substantially-balanced economy, with the supply-side process spurring the exceptional progress. There was balance in government generally, doing those things required to support the free-market structure and little more. Under such conditions the private sector also experienced a generally-balanced existence. It produced not only enough for its own needs but also sold and exported abroad many of our products and services. And the less affluent knew there was always a great opportunity for them to advance. For the poor and needy, society provided a compassionate safety net.

The rich in this country long have engaged in conspicuous consumption. What we have seen in these past few decades is the middle class acting as they, too, are rich by consuming more than they can afford. We used to throw banquets but now we sit at a lunch counter scratching to pay the check, relying on other nations to pay the tab. We used to be a creditor nation but now we are a debtor nation. And this applies to both the private and the public sectors.

Our welfare state has supplied much on both sides of this formula; it has widely restricted production and encouraged consumption. Here our tax structure is a major contributor, and this is intensified by the entitlement benefits being paid to many millions. Stifling government regulations are also major contributors. Consuming huge amount of energy, we could easily become energy self-sufficient, but we now import each year a trillion dollars worth of petroleum products, seven percent of our GDP. We permit OPEC to monopolize and set monopoly prices, and quietly accept this huge factor in the production-consumption formula, not even trying to set up an OPIC (Organization of Petroleum Importing Countries) to contradict it. We rely on China and other countries not only to flood this country with consumer and other good but we also rely on them as major providers of credit, as they constantly buy and hold huge amounts of U.S. Treasury obligations.

What are we doing about this deplorable and unacceptable situation? It would seem very little. Our government does not give a full account of our national debt. Official statistics acknowledge the roughly $16 trillion in debt originating mostly from cumulative federal deficits. They do not tell us of the at least $60 trillion in long-term liabilities, principally in Social Security and Medicare, that will only widen further once the Obama health care reforms take full effect. This will heighten consumption without the means to pay for it. The government also uses the budget to hide the truth, using a consolidated budget in which the operational deficits cash flows are offset by the cash coming in for the entitlements.

To underline some of the foregoing, I quote from a January 30, 2012 letter to The Claremont Institute:

"In 2012, our generation stands at a crossroad. What legacy will we leave our children and grandchildren?

- Constitutional government or an unchecked, tyrannical bureaucracy?
- Free enterprise and job creation or a weak socialist economy?
- Self-evident truths or the abyss of moral relativism?
- Individual rights or class warfare?
- Liberty and self-reliance or slavish government dependency?
- "The answers to these questions-and more-are very much in doubt."
- And from a letter of January 31, 2011 to the Institute for Energy Research:

"First, Americans are tired - sick to death, even - of energy prices they know are artificially high. They know the economy could grow if the price of gas, of heating fuel and of transportation were not hobbling you and me and the businesses we rely on to fuel our American economy."

"Second,, More and more Americans are learning the truth about the Far-Left's anti-American energy Green Mythology. They're seeing boondoggles like Solyndra and so many others for what they are. And they've had enough."

"Third, Americans are waking up to the fact of American Energy Abundance! We have uncovered the amazing truth that America can provide all the secure, affordable energy she needs from her own reserves.... For generations and generations to come...."

We have been witnessing a true tragedy in financial management of this country by our government, Federal and State. We are approaching national bankruptcy. We certainly need bold, practical plans right now to turn this around.

Our monstrous debts must be confronted, all of them. We must intelligently plan how to handle them even before we can begin to talk about any kind of balancing. How should we best handle them? We all know they are our debts, they accrued on our watch. Repayment must be made as default is out of the question.

Here is a practical, hard-headed solution. We must gradually transfer these debts from the public to the private sector, for ultimately it is the private sector that must pay. In the transfer process, we can get reasonable control of it.

Under this approach, people would be permitted to choose those entitlement benefits they really want and can afford; that alone will cut the debt and increase the efficiency, while at the same time flowing these funds into investments, providing capital needed by our growing industries. This saving and investment has been fatally absent from our economy for too long. Thus through privatization people will own their retirement income and health saving plans, and at the same time, help provide needed capital. Elimination of the trillions of dollars of payroll taxes as huge charges against production will free-up and make available that which has been sorely lacking. At the same time, of course, the operations of the governments at the federal, state and local levels must be reduced to levels that are constitutional and necessary.

But under this privatized system, the people will be owed a moral if not legal obligation a refund of the vast sums that they have paid in and which have been diverted to many purposes other than funding entitlements. This can be measured and equitably returned to each person.

This, of course, will require a substantial surtax for many years (thus paying our penance for letting this happen), and this tax should be designed at the same time to decrease consumption and increase production. A national sales tax, superimposed upon all state sales taxes, would be the logical vehicle, with the Federal government sending back to the states their portions. Such a program would give back much of our lost freedom. Yet it does not address the main problem: the federal monopoly over our currency, banking and credit system. This, too, must be privatized.

This brief chapter has presented a major problem hanging over this country as well as a general indication of how we can proceed to solve it. It is a major challenge. It will require tremendous work.

CHAPTER ELEVEN

AN UNBALANCED COUNTRY.
A DETAILED LISTING OF ITS PROBLEMS

The preceding chapter discussed the problems of our country in urgent need of correction. While there is general agreement that things must change, there is widespread disagreement over how this can be achieved. In these pages, I am sketching out some solutions. For an understanding of how we got to this point, it will be helpful to take a look at our history following the Civil War.

The Republican Party was founded in 1854, seven years before the war began. With the Union victory in 1865, the party ruled for most of the time through 1932. The country was heavily engaged in territorial expansion, both in the continental U.S. and abroad. While this posed problems, it did not threaten the prevailing free market. And there was plenty of land for which European immigrants could settle. The main political grievances in domestic policy centered upon metal: whether or not our dollar should be backed by gold or silver.

The turning point came during the second decade of the 20th century. The enactment of the Federal Reserve System and the income tax amendment laid the groundwork for our current problems. This was masked during the high-growth 1920s, but came back to haunt the nation with the onset of the Great Depression in the early 1930s. The longtime Secretary of the Treasury, Andrew Mellon, eventually resigned because his sound advice was not heeded.

Under Franklin Delano Roosevelt, the Great Depression did not end. Indeed, it continued longer than it should have. This is because he, his key advisers and many in Congress regarded the Constitution as out of date. World War II provided the illusion of solving the problem. Yes, we did win. But we racked up enormous debt in the process. After the War, the country became preoccupied with rebuilding our own country and the nations of Western Europe. The Truman, Eisenhower and Kennedy years saw an aggressive expansion of government. The turning point occurred in the mid-Sixties during the administration of President Lyndon B. Johnson. Congress, at his urging, passed Medicare and expanded any number of social welfare entitlement programs. The Nixon and Ford administrations may have been Republican, but they did not roll back government in any meaningful sense. Jimmy Carter ran as a "good government" reformer, but his main legacy, aside from leaving our country dangerously exposed to Soviet and Islamic aggression, was to create high inflation and unemployment, coupled with more government intervention in the economy.

The eight years under President Ronald Reagan offered some respite, but government grew during his tenure as well. The first Bush administration reversed much of the progress in shrinking the State, a process Bill Clinton expanded, though thankfully restrained to a degree by the Republican-controlled Congress elected in 1994. And government grew even more rapidly under Republican George W. Bush, who somehow could not bring himself to veto a single spending or authorization bill. That brings us to President Obama. Though calling for "change" throughout his 2008 presidential campaign, what he meant was more of the same, only harder and faster. His proposed massive health care overhaul, which Congress passed in 2010, thanks to some rather blatant parliamentary sleight of hand inflicted by Senate Majority Leader Harry Reid, may prove to be the most dangerous piece of legislation in our nation's history.

I am, by nature, an optimist. Indeed, optimism has kept me happy and healthy for more than 100 years. But I have an old friend who breathes and thrives on pessimism. For example, he claims that the happy ending in the Book of Job was an editing correction needed to make the Bible a "best seller" because there was already too much doom and gloom in the Old Testament and the original ending was just too much. It would make sense here to quote him here.

A Soliloquy and Sad Summary Where We Stand Today.

- Stupidity has become institutionalized and all of us are now living in that institution run by the government.

- Statesmanship now is simply the dreaming of politicians who are trying to escape the nightmare of the people in pursuit. This is the black art practiced on the Potomac and is drowned well before floating past Mount Vernon, leaving a skeleton that has now been left for the seagulls to pick.

- The low-calorie gruel that is now being ground in the grist-mill of Big Government can be clearly seen when we compare it with the high-calorie fare we had during the period when the free-market system was given a chance to operate and produced bountiful results.

- Big Government brags that it has taken all the steps necessary for all markets to work perfectly but people cannot make trades or buy anything without paying the government a royalty, plus first checking to see if they can legally make it.

- Big Government lauds loudly free competition while at the same time stifling it. It permits and supports private monopolies. In money and credit, it fantasizes that the Federal Reserve System can help, but it operates only to perpetuate the credit monopoly it exercises over business with the help of the Big Banks, making them too big to fail, and when failing revives them, and prescribes the same medicine for the next time they will fail. Big Government fails to realize that for the private sector to operate effectively, it must have freedom to operate these essential service functions.

- The prostitution of private ownership of property is part of this parody and parade. The once sacred right of ownership of property by the people has been completely decimated, and owners must pay repeatedly for any rights of ownership and "peaceful possession" of that which they thought was guaranteed to them.

- Big Government has raped and exterminated solid economics. It is now an upside-down-world of supply and demand. It believes the people can eat food before it is produced. Money which of course has no value magically gains value if enough of it is printed! That Big Government "Demand" and "Supply" has no substance is ignored. But it continues to write this graffiti and nonsense on all public walls for all to see.

The foregoing is what my impatient and pessimistic pal has been pointing out, and certainly an abundance of truth shines through all this sarcasm. I admit that my optimism cannot begin to rebut and dispel all of this gloom.

I should like to be a modern Paul Revere riding a horse, swinging a lantern, shouting that the redcoats are coming. But I am too late in doing that; the redcoats are already here, have stolen my steed, and although I still have my lantern, it is empty and I cannot afford to fill it as they have driven the price of fuel too high. In view of this dismal scene, I don't even want to visit Boston, one of my favorite cities.

My old friend, of course, is right on most of this. There is no need for me to supply a big basket full of statistics to support that; the reader need but look at the daily paper and listen to all of the other media to see overwhelming support. As an antidote to pessimism, I recommend several books published by Cato Institute scholars, offering a short summary of each:

"The Dirty Dozen: How Twelve Supreme Court Cases Radically Expanded Government and Eroded Freedom." Written by Robert Levy and William Mellor, this is an essential piece of reading. It analyzes major Supreme Court decisions over the decades that have significantly eroded individual liberties and constitutional government.

"The Politics of Freedom: Taking on the Left, the Right, and Threats to our Liberties." One of the leading libertarian commentators in the nation, David Boaz, offers his unique and often surprising views on such hot-button issues as federal spending, individual rights, drugs, immigration, and the war on terror, education, and government intrusion into private lives.

"The Cult of the Presidency: America's Dangerous Devotion to Executive Power." This acclaimed book by Gene Healy reveals how Americans have expanded presidential power over recent decades by expecting solutions for all national problems and concludes by calling for the president's role to return to its properly-defined constitutional limits.

"The Right to Earn a Living: Economic Freedom and the Law." Author Timothy Sandefur argues that America's founders thought the right to earn a living was so basic that it didn't need to be mentioned in the Bill of Rights. The author takes reader through the history of the right to earn a living and the many ways that burdensome government laws, regulations and court decisions threaten that right today.

"Liberty of Contract: Rediscovering a Lost Constitutional Right." David Mayer charts the history of the fundamental human right of economic liberty and shows how this right has been continuously diminished by controversial court rulings and our country's growing regulatory and welfare state.

"Financial Fiasco: How America's Infatuation with Homeownership and Easy Money Created the Economic Crisis." An easily accessible work on the economic crisis, Johan Norberg guides the reader through the irresponsible behavior by the financial industry, backed by an implicit "too big to fail" government guarantee, and why this was primarily responsible for the collapse of 2008 and its after-effects. Norberg argues that we are continuing to repeat these mistakes today.

CHAPTER TWELVE

The Abomination That Is Taxes. A Constitutional Internal Revenue Code

Article I.
Section. 8. The congress shall have Power to
lay and collect Taxes, Duties, Imposts and Excises,
to pay the Debts and provide for the common
Defence and general Welfare of the United States;
but all Duties, imposts and excises shall be uniform
throughout the United States.

Article I,
Section 9. The Privilege of the Writ of Habeas Corpus
shall not be suspended, unless when in Cases of
Rebellion or Invasion the public Safety may require it.
No Bill of Attainder or ex post facto Law shall be passed.
No Capitation, or other direct, Tax shall be laid,
unless in Proportion to the Census or Enumeration
herein before directed to be taken.

AMENDMENT XVI
The Congress shall have power to lay and collect
taxes on incomes, from whatever source derived,

> without apportionment among the several
> States, and without regard to any census or
> enumeration.

One of my earliest problems, at age six, was with taxes, and it involved a 20 percent rate. I started my schooling in a one-room country schoolhouse in 1918. Although this was well before teachers unions, there was a teacher-board conflict. The result was that in mid-year the teacher quit. I then went to the village school where one of my sisters was teaching the intermediate grades. One noon she gave me a nickel to buy an ice cream cone, and so I went across the street to the drug store. When I offered my nickel, Mr. Nulle, the druggist, informed me that another war tax had been levied, imposing a penny tax on the cone. But because my credit was good, he let me keep it anyway. Embarrassed but still licking the cone, I returned to the school and informed my sister of my problem, whereupon she gave me a penny and I went back and paid my debt. Unfortunately, our government has a less responsible approach to paying its debts.

This country was born in conflict over taxes, with the Stamp Act and other enactments of "taxation without representation." Thus was born the Boston Tea Party and deep disaffection with George III. And after achieving independence, President George Washington's first problems were with taxes. Faced with the Whiskey Rebellion in 1794, he used troops to collect a tax. And thus it has been ever since.

The language in Article I, Section 8 of the Constitution quoted above is straightforward. Taxes to be levied are to "provide for the common Defence and general Welfare of the United States." This meant the the government, not the people. The uniformity requirement resulted in much debate. In 1913, when the income tax amendment was passed, it was not only to clarify this, but also to raise funds for new operations of the government.

In the long term, taxes are the costs of government; these costs should be relatively modest under peace-time conditions. But when the costs of government exceed the tax revenues, it is mandatory that this excess must be reduced. This out-of-balance condition spinning out of control harms everybody and must be fixed lest we face fiscal devastation. When this unacceptable condition is further worsened by so-called entitlements that are not funded or voluntary, this becomes totally intolerable.

In the century since the passage of the 16th amendment, this country and its Congress have forgotten its precise meaning. We have taxes on all manner of things beyond personal income. And now we have Supreme Court discovering that we can be taxed not only for things we buy, but also for things we don't buy. This authority goes well beyond the spirit of the Constitution.

There is entirely too much confusion about taxes – why they are needed, their legal basis, method of administration, and overall impact. Taxes are needed to the extent they cover the costs of governing. If tax requirements cannot be met, government should not be enlarged at any level.

First of all we need a quantitative assessment of where we are. The Tax Foundation, a widely respected nonpartisan think tank around for about 75 years, provides an excellent summary. As an educational nonprofit, members are frequently called upon to testify before Congress and state legislatures, also in the courts. In September 2012, it released facts and figures from the Internal Revenue Service for 2009. These numbers support the assertion that the United States has the most progressive federal income tax system in the industrial world.

Here are the most crucial facts of the Foundation's analysis:

- *Top 1% of all taxpayer pay more in income taxes that the bottom 90% (those making under $120,000)*
- *Top 0.1% of all taxpayers pay more than the bottom 75% combined*
- *Top 1% of all taxpayers earn 16% of our country's income, yet pays 36% of federal income taxes.*
- *Top 3% of all taxpayers pay half of federal income taxes*
- *Roughly 59 million individual tax filers pay no federal income tax*
- *Roughly 23 million individual tax filers receive a refundable tax credit greater than what they pay in federal income and payroll taxes (16 million including the employer portion of payroll taxes)*
- *Average effective tax rate (ET.R) of all taxpayer is 11 %*
- *Average ETR of the top 1% of taxpayers is 24%*
- *Average ETR of all millionaires is 25%*
- *Roughly half of American household pay no federal income tax* includes household not required to file a tax return*

Here is the factual summarization of corporate facts and figures for 2009:

- *Top U.S. federal statutory corporate tax rate is 35%, giving us the highest rate in the industrialized world*
- *Federal effective tax rate (ETR) for all corporations is 26% (including Foreign Taxes Paid, the effective rate jumps to 33%)*
- *In addition to roughly $300 billion in federal income taxes, U.S. corporations paid nearly $100 billion in income taxes to foreign government and roughly $200 billion in other domestic taxes*

- *Approximate total tax preferences available in current tax code are:*
    Roughly $100 billion for corporations
    Roughly $900 billion for individuals

- *Let's put tax preferences in perspective:*
    Exclusion for health coverage - $174 billion
    Exclusion for pension and 401K's - $136 billion
    All corporate tax expenditures "loopholes" - $103 billion
    Mortgage interest deduction - $89 billion

- *Of the $103 billion of tax preferences for corporation:*
    $69 billion is available to ALL industries
    $17 billion are industry specific - some examples:
    Expenditures for Coal and Minerals - $1.3 billion
    Expenditures for "Renewable" - $1.8 billion
    Expenditures for Oil and Gas - $2.2 billion

- *More business income (57%) is taxed under the individual tax code than the corporate tax code*

The Tower of Babel that is taxes today. Taxes deservedly are receiving a lot of public attention. But the discussions are inconclusive because there are many kinds of taxes, each with their own effect on individuals and businesses.

Property taxes are on wealth. To hold there should be a direct federal tax on property, i.e. on wealth, would not only be duplicative but would also be unconstitutional, certainly lacking uniformity. Yet this contradicts Amendment XVI, passed in 1913, which states: "The Congress shall have power to lay and collect taxes on incomes, from whatever source derived...." In other words, the amendment does not authorize a tax on property or other assets.

Aside from being unconstitutional, most taxes are contrary to Christian principles. firmly believes that we should render unto Caesar what is Caesar's, but overlooks that we should render unto God what is God's and to God's people. (Reference: Matthew 22, v21.) He believes and orders we should render everything unto Caesar and then let the socialist Caesar decide on not only the pittance to go to the people but also who should receive that pittance.

Matthew speaks to that which is the peoples (Ch. 20, v 15) "Is it not lawful for me to do what I will with my own? Is thine eye evil because I am good?" President Reagan, who had been a Sunday school teacher, may have used this sense of evil when he referred to the Soviet as being an evil empire.

What today must we render unto Caesar? Speaking in many tongues, there is much confusion. The income tax law under which much of the Bush tax cuts expired on December 31, 2012, leaves a void. After a "Decade of Change"*, we are in a never-never land where all businesses in the private sector cannot plan. No wonder we are lacking that essential confidence that is needed for a healthy economy and growth.

---

* A Decade of Change. A decade of tax cuts began with the Economic Growth and Tax Relief Reconciliation Act of 2001 (P.L. 107-16), which reflected congressional compromises on tax rate reduction, estate tax repeal, marriage penalty relief education incentives, child tax credit increase, pension reform, and alternative minimum tax relief. However, to meet budgetary constraints, provisions are phased in and out over the next 10 years, with an anticipated sunset in 2011 that would reinstate the Code as it was prior to this enactment. 2009 U.S. Master Tax Guide

Before becoming a disciple, Matthew was a tax collector, and he knew very well he could not collect taxes where there was no wherewithal. Caesar can take only where the consumption is less than the production, with production coming first. "Give us this day our daily bread!" In the Old Testament, the book of Deuteronomy can be considered the gospel of entitlements, where our Lord promises us all kinds of benefits if we are good but much harm if we are bad. It has been called the Book of Blessings and Curses. But we must look to Matthew for how we can earn our entitlements, preaching with parables and principles that man has a duty to be diligent and to use all his talents, skills and energy in producing that which is good and needed. Those who are deficient in this are termed "the least of these" (which too often is interpreted as meaning "the poor"--a gross error made by 4,000 ministers who ran a full-page advertisement in a Washington newspaper in July 2011!).

We should be very suspicious of a person who claims he had regularly worshipped under the guidance of Reverend Wright, who was not only located on the south side of Chicago but who also was on the south side of conventional Christian teaching.

Obama apparently never read the New Testament and must have just skimmed through the Old Testament. Today, he thinks bishops are to be recognized when playing chess. This is a country based on a Judeo-Christian heritage. But Socialism is a negation of these principles. For this nation to receive the blessings set forth in Deuteronomy we must follow the message of Matthew if we are to earn those blessings. Our leadership must be dedicated to this in both thoughts and actions.

Coming down to earth, here is what now confronts us. One of the unquestioned needs for taxes is to cover not only present spending but previous government overspending. That is now acknowledged by the government in only a very small fraction of the total, being Treasury obligations now outstanding. But real debt is about four times greater when we calculate the present value of long-term government liabilities. The real sum, in fact, is over $60 trillion, and growing. This debt will be inherited by our children and grandchildren. It is of the greatest importance that we recognize it now and take strong steps to deal with it. It is sovereign debt upon which we cannot default. Orderly liquidation must be firmly established.

We are now being pushed down the road to socialism under President Obama, who is positioning himself as an American Caesar.

The Sixteenth Amendment Explained and Defined.

This is to state and emphasize what the income tax amendment did and did not do.

This amendment, as it plainly says in a few words, did only one thing: It gave the federal government the power to tax income. It did not give the Congress the power to define what income really is or what it would like it to be. It did not give the Congress more legitimate purposes than it already had; it only widened the base for proper taxation to income. It definitely did not take away from the people their inalienable rights set forth in the Declaration and guaranteed by the Constitution.

The Founders certainly did not go to the trouble of writing the Constitution in order to make it changeable on a whim by Congress. And to make that very clear, included in it in Article I, Section 9, are these: "No Bill of Attainder shall be passed", and "The Privilege of the Writ of Habeas Corpus shall not be suspended unless when in Cases of Rebellion or Invasion the Public Safety may require it." Some jurists and others have argued that Amendment IX expands significantly the powers of Congress when it says: "The enumeration in the Constitution of certain rights shall not be construed to deny or disparage other retained by the people", but those raising questions overlook completely that the rights retained by the people are on much solider grounds as pointed out above. No self-serving legislation or even an amendment could do that. Any such legislation would amount to a denial of the Writ of Habeas Corpus and would constitute an unconstitutional Bill of Attainder.

What is income? What is taxable income? According to Webster's Dictionary, income is "something that comes in as addition; that gain or recurrent benefit (usually measured in money) which proceeds from labor, business, or property." There can be little doubt that it was this second part that was the intent behind the income tax authorization. It was what man does when he "earns his daily bread", and not in his everyday personal activities. Income is strictly an economic term, a concept, and must be so understood and used. Accordingly, we should look to sound and simple principles of taxation that would reflect for each person the ability to pay as well as the relative benefits conferred to the person by the operations of government. This justifies moderate progressivity in its impact, principally the rate schedule.

Here are some more common-sense observations in the enactment and administration of income taxes on the people. They should be simple, easily understood and easily calculated. They should not be duplicative; income taxed once should not be taxed again to the same taxpayer, and he should be required to calculate it only once and not in alternate ways. And the taxpayer should not have to pay any of the tax before the income is actually earned and received. But our present administrative practice and Code violates all of these reasonable standards for fair taxation. This is universally recognized but there has been no urgency to make those major changes that are clearly called for.

The history of income taxes in the United States. Without the 1913 amendment, Congress perhaps thought it had the authority to enact an income tax of sort but it would have had a very unsound basis because of the recognized requirement for uniformity in federal taxes, and there was much discussion on this. Remember, the Founders in order to hold down the size of government, wanted such taxes to directly hit the individual. In this way, there people would have a built-in incentive to oppose their being raised.

An income tax, in fact, was imposed during the Civil War but was allowed to lapse after the Union victory in 1865. In the 1880s another such tax was passed, but in 1895 the Supreme Court "refused the idea" and reinvigorated the direct-tax clauses, holding the tax was direct and not properly apportioned. Thereafter, it was decided that enacting a new income tax law would be too risky politically. In 1909, supporters of an income tax chose to amend the Constitution and four years later realized their objective. The states should have been more insistent on adding qualifying language to the amendment.

The Supreme Court has had no recent cases to articulate a more precise meaning of this amendment or to even consider what broadening might be reasonable and acceptable. Unfortunately, the general understanding these days is that Congress has plenary powers over taxation, and that Congress itself has very broad power over what can be reached by the income tax, in both what taxable income is and what can be deducted from it, or made entirely free from any tax.

Other considerations. "Fairness" in taxation. The Death Tax.

Other than the routine buying and selling in our daily activities providing for our personal needs, there are other exchange transactions in the market place involving capital goods. This free flow is an essential part of our system, facilitating the transfers of such goods and services to where they are more urgently needed. Any taxation on them must be kept low. But under current income tax law, they are taxed as capital gains, where the amount received exceeds the "cost basis" of that sold, thus taxable as income. Such exchanges of equal values are taxed as capital gains, usually at 15 percent. But where there are net capital losses, they are allowed against income up to only $3,000. There is no justification or fairness in this. Further, to the extent the "gain" may be attributable to government-sponsored inflation, it is morally wrong. It has resulted in needless political infighting.

Also deserving close Constitutional scrutiny is another law-- the "Estate, Gift and Generation-Skipping Transfer Tax", a unified TRANSFER TAX SYSTEM ON THE TRANSFER OF PROPERTY UPON DEATH. This is assessed against the estate of the deceased person but in effect is really paid by the heirs and beneficiaries before the estate is disbursed. This is a direct tax on them. It certainly is not apportioned in accordance with the population of "the several States."

The Federal Insurance Contribution Act. Initiated in 1935, an employer was required to withhold social security taxes from wages paid and must also match the tax withheld. In 1975 this was extended to hospital and medical expenses, and in 2003 to prescription drugs, plus some modifications for health-savings accounts, extending into the states. Although the Act refers to these as "Contributions", they are generally called "Taxes", with the

Supreme Court using that term prominently in its 2012 Obamacare decision.

There is little if any Constitutional basis for the federal government to impose such taxes directly on the people, and worse, to force employers match it. The natural inalienable rights included in the Constitution as its sound base consists first of all of man's rights over his own life, over his own body, and to do that responsibly, including taking care of his needs which also certainly include provisions for life after being unable to work any more, plus his health throughout his life. By imposing these heavy taxes, the federal government has deprived him of his means to do much of this. Vital and essential parts of his freedom have been taken from him. And in the process as set forth in other sections of this book, the federal government has withdrawn from the productive factors of the private sector very substantial resources so that now it cannot begin to produce all that is required for consumption. All of this is not only unconstitutional but is a crime against the soul and dignity of man, making him a slave and serf of others claiming to represent the sovereign government!

The Patient Protection and Affordable Care Act ("Obamacare").

Lastly, I look at this unbelievable legislation which is just about as bad as it can get. For many reasons, it does not even approach being constitutional. It is a wholesale denial and violation of those inalienable natural rights of man set forth and guaranteed by the Constitution, specifically:

- It is not understandable. The shock of the justices upon their first look at the sheer volume of the law, over 2,600 pages, was clearly evident. Then had they discharge their full judicial duty (as set forth in another chapter hereof), the Court would have voided it without any further examination.

- It violates the rights of the free person that we have to take care of our own body, our right to life, and thus over all aspects of our health and well-being.

- It violates our unquestioned right to make contracts with other persons, and to look to the government for enforcement. Here a so-called insurance contract was being forced upon free man.

- This was a fraud upon each person when it was presented as "insurance", which it clearly is not. Insurance, the exercise of personal contractual rights, has been a valuable institution practiced for centuries wherein man contracts to transfer those risks he foresees that his financial resources will not cover to another party with adequate resources, who agrees to accept and make whole those risks for an agreed upon "premium." In this so-called insurance, the federal government does not contract or guarantee against these casualties, but instead it sets forth a number or vague promises how it might if it wished take care of them. The "premium" was the vague and unlimited right of the government to impose taxes on everybody to cover. This is not insurance.

- The Act provides that if the person decides to uphold and maintain his rights not to enter into such an outrageous arrangement, then he would be assessed a fine, a fine that the Supreme Court reached out to call a "tax". Here Justice

Roberts and the Court reached out far into the omnibus, "grab-bag", which the power to tax has become, thus usurping the Constitution.

A Constitutional Internal Revenue Code.

Taxable income for such individuals will consist of that person's economic income--income from labor, business, property, etc. It will also include but only to the extent the present language of the Constitution permits it, including uniformity, many items of personal income and expenses--interest and dividend income, deductions for local and state taxes, etc. Such items like capital gains, interest expenses, medical expenses, and various losses and gains will require further study.

A major change will be that charitable contributions of all kinds and of all amounts will no longer be deductible from taxable income. There is no support for that in the document, but there of course there is always much support from politicians running for election. The Bible says that almsgiving is good when it comes from the heart but otherwise it may be questionable. The Code generally approves of giving but only some of it is good enough to qualify as a deduction!

Much has and can be written about charitable contributions. They are voluntary and optional expenditures and much of their real "goodness" is a matter of individual evaluation. There are no solid reasons why they should be related to the taxes our federal government should raise for its operations, and there are many good reasons why these contributions should not be tax-advantaged. This reform will eliminate much current and mostly meaningless discussion when comparing the tax rates paid by different and particularly affluent people.

There are also some other substantial benefits that will result. Some charitable institutions have thrived and grown so large, and much of this growth can perhaps be ascribed to the tax deductibility and not on true merit, so they have attained outsized influence and economic power, and secondly, as most communities exempt such property from local taxation, many have become so large that they have become a burden on the rest of the community. This new reform policy will conform more closely with Judeo-Christian morality and culture. Further, to the extent that income should be redistributed, this is the way much of it should be handled, with much better results than when the flawed and costly heavy hands of government manage the process. Further, with more efficient allocation of resources, even marginally, the productivity of the private sector will get a big boost.

Finally, too much of the urge among those building the present tax system has had the objective of maximizing taxes whereas our Constitution clearly says that is completely wrong.

PRINCIPLES FOR THE FEDERAL TAXATION OF THE PEOPLE

- Taxes must cover the reasonable and legitimate cost of operating the government. Where this has not been enough, current taxes must include enough to cover these debts.

- Taxes levied upon its people cannot take from them their inalienable rights guaranteed them by the Constitution.

- Taxes levied upon its people can be for only those purposes set forth in the Constitution.

- Acceptable principles of taxation should be used and this requires recognition of personal ability to pay as well as personal benefits received from the government. This justifies a moderate degree of progressivity in rates.

- The income tax imposed by the 16th amendment is on personal economic income and must be levied accordingly. Only negative economic income can be deducted from that. Accordingly, charitable contributions are not deductible except where directly related to taxable income. The income tax is on the person, and each person is responsible for compliance.

- Operations of nonprofit institutions are exempt from income taxes on their charitable operations. They must look to their own revenues for the support of their existence.

- Where people combine to form corporations, their composite income cannot be taxed in excess of the individual rates because that would be a penalty for combining. As a practical matter, corporation tax rates must approximate that of it shareholder's paying the lower rates.

- Where corporations pay dividends to shareholder, that comes from income already taxed and should not be taxed again.

- Proper and efficient methods should be used in the levying and collection of taxes. The present methods are not only burdensome, costly and inefficient but they are in violations of our civil rights. Taxes on income should not be payable until they are earned.

- To the extent that capital gains are income they should be taxed as income but to the extent they result from government sponsored inflation they should be exempt. The practical solution is to tax them at lower rates.

Conclusion: To the extent that the Internal Revenue Code is in direct conflict with the above, it must be revised and reformed. This country cannot operate in direct violation of its Constitution. Further, taxes can be levied and permitted to cover only the essential and legal activities of government at all levels. Finally, as all taxes ultimately are born by the people, their inalienable rights cannot be violated.

How can we handle the major emergency of correcting this?

The foregoing establishes that we have a very serious problem in that the Internal Revenue Code and other taxation laws are in violation of the Constitution. Having faith that this country will insist on law and order and not anarchy, we assume that we have the capacity to face the situation forthrightly.

We cannot very well look to a Congress that has been blithely passing such laws without glancing at the Constitution. Nor can we look to presidential administrations complicit in these actions. But as set forth in the chapter, "The Complete Supreme Court," we might look to the Court to order legislative action. Failing that, the states might rise up and call for a Constitutional Convention to initiate amendments to clarify and make right these inalienable rights of the people. That convention would call on the Supreme Court to actively engage these activities, stamping its approval on all of their final actions.

In the meantime, however, this country would be in turmoil; without money, the federal government cannot function. So extraordinary actions and extreme patience will be required. The Supreme Court may even have to ask the president to deny a Writ of Writs of Habeas Corpus to cope with a potential breakdown of government.

What would prompt the states to call a convention? All of them have had to comply with unsustainable federal mandates. Then, too, we must look to the states and the people to be most understanding; in the common interest they will voluntarily want to get together on a nonpartisan basis to meet this unprecedented emergency. The private sector, too long ignored, will then start to regain its proper and indispensable place. The philosophy of free-market capitalism will be seen as the savior of the country, and will again have an opportunity to flourish. The members of this ad hoc Convention will look, of course, to the private sector for support and guidance, with a much smaller government bound to emerge.

With such internal turmoil, disorder and confusion, this country would be vulnerable to all kinds of foreign threats and forces, and our citizens would certainly respond with a new-found patriotism. So out of all this turbulence, a new country might emerge.

Much patience and understanding would be required from all of the people if an orderly transition were to be achieved, and this should be expected. Taxpayers might well agree to continue to pay taxes following a formula based on what they had been paying, receiving credits for these taxes paid which would then be applied to actual taxes due as finally correctly determined. These credits would be guaranteed to be honored when the new legal and equitable taxation is again made the law of the land.

The foregoing represents an impossible situation. When this is recognized by a clear majority of Americans, we then will be ready to institute the only fair and constitutional solution – the privatization of retirement accounts, health care, banking, credit and money, as set forth later in the book.

CHAPTER THIRTEEN

A LETTER TO THE NATION UPON MY ONE HUNDREDTH BIRTHDAY

To the nation:

I write this upon my one hundredth birthday. I write it not as a Republican or a Democrat or as an Independent. My only allegiance is to my country.

Today, I am deeply alarmed about the future of this once great country. Starting in 1776, we established a sound basis for its governance, a government of, by and for the people, recognizing all the rights with which our Creator endowed us, subject only to those limited laws needed to protect us in a civil society.

For years, everything functioned very well within that framework. But in the past 100 years, this has deteriorated, and we now face a complete breakdown. This has principally been caused by an expanding government that has taken from us many of these rights, all under the delusion that this would benefit and strengthen all. In this, we have seen it is a complete failure. This should be no surprise as history has clearly shown that the socialist state has harmed more than it has helped. But today too many of us are still laboring under the same destructive delusion.

Many of us have been calling loudly for the government to correct itself but without agreement. The cause of this is extreme, bitter partisanship, starting with the people themselves and blooming fully in the Federal government. With this deplorable condition, it is no longer possible for this country to function as it was designed to do, and with that failure come accelerating abandonment of our rights. Clearly something must be done, and the logical thing to correct this is to remove that cause--extreme partisanship.

This extreme partisanship has us at the crossroads; we have an incompatible, non-functioning system of government. If we want to maintain a constitutional government, we must take steps such as I have outlined, and that will require that we make fully effective our system of checks-and-balances among the three branches of government. That means we must remove from the membership of the Supreme Court any taint of partisanship, so it can perform its sole duty as set forth in Article III--"The Judicial Power of the United States shall be vested in one supreme Court, and in such inferior Courts as the Congress may from time to time ordain and establish."

The membership now over time shifts with the political party in control, and consequently we have a politicized court so that it cannot possible discharge its true judicial function. Over time, with the presidency and the congress sanitized from this extreme partisanship, the Court itself would become sanitized.

This intense partisanship could continue to flourish at the state level, but when the states see what beneficial results can be accomplished at the Federal level, they undoubtedly would take positive steps to curb it. There undoubtedly would emerge many small parties, but that is the essence of democracy.

It is long past due for this country to take positive, strong steps to resolve this fatal impasse. Both presidential candidates, in fact all candidates for public office, should be required to answer this question: *Do you want free markets or do you want socialism?* This would force the liberals to face up to reality; can they prove that it can produce the quality of life, the balance between materialism and freedom that we have clearly seen in our past history that has been exceptional when our constitutional system of government has been given the opportunity to flourish? Do we want rank materialism or a fuller life?

President Obama should take another look at the Lord's Prayer. He should note, as we all do, that we cannot eat that "daily bread" until it is produced, and only the people can produce it, and if properly motivated they can produce large and copious quantities. Fully one half of that Prayer is asking our fellow man for compassion and that we not be tempted to reach for more than we have earned and deserve. Further, the giving of alms is good if from the heart, but otherwise if what is ours is taken from us; those people forcing this are "evil". That is the immorality of socialism!

Obama is totally unrealistic. It is obvious that when we render everything to that Caesar that is our Federal government, and he seizes it and grabs for more, then there will be nothing left, and the economy will constantly be going downhill. As more and more people receive their "daily bread" without working for it, the quantity of it will be compoundingly diminishing, until there is not bread for anyone, including Caesar and his soldiers. Then the protestors, the barbarians (now at the 'gate), will move in and take over. Even the peaceful Tea Partyers will join in (and they have guns, thanks to the Second Amendment.) The "serfs" then will have become barbarians. Finally, all will have equality--the equality of poverty and starvation, the equality of nothingness.

In Federalist 63, James Madison looked to save us always "the cool and deliberate sense of the community." He hoped they would take over. For this to happen, we must now implement strong and positive, in fact revolutionary, steps to remedy this impasse, hoping we still have that "cool and deliberate" sense.

CHAPTER FOURTEEN

THE BUDGET AND THE CONSTITUTION

There is nothing in the Constitution referring directly to budgets. But unquestionably it calls for strong fiscal controls and discipline over public monies. Article I, Section 8 says:

"No Money shall be drawn from the Treasury but in Consequence of Appropriations made by Law; and a regular Statement and Account of the Receipts and Expenditures of all public Money shall be published from time to time."

Prudent management of these appropriations calls for planning, particularly as the Constitution is very stingy in the amount of government that is to be permitted. Further, it is the clear duty of Congress to provide funds for all three branches of government, with each branch having enough to discharge its designated duties. It is only this ability that makes the built-in system of checks and balances so effective. It's the key to our democratic form of government if the people are to govern themselves.

What should a budget be? A budget should be an honest estimate of appropriations for the next fiscal year under current law, plus some recognition of prospective laws where there is a real possibility for enactment soon. If those drafting the budget favor strongly other legislation, they can at most be footnotes. Budgets must be on the cash and accrual basis. Each year's projected expenditures should show that year's portion of future cash spending already passed, such as "entitlements" which must be fully included.

Without deep digging, each budget should be understandable by all. This means there must be more than one budget where appropriations extend beyond those for the operations for limited and proper government. Where laws have been passed for other than this, such as the "entitlements," separate budgets are a necessity. The confusion of consolidated budgets should be barred absolutely.

All parties should show their sincerity in upholding the Constitution by joining to pass firm legislation making a precondition the passage of a budget before any laws can be passed by that Congress. Budgets should originate in the House, as always has been the case, but the Senate has a joint responsibility here. As the president will be called upon to administer the budget, his cooperation in the process is very much in order.

The budget is a Constitutional requirement, and if it is the honest intent to govern in accordance with its provisions, budgets must be prepared and passed.

PART 3

PUTTING THE CONSTITUTION TO WORK FIXING AMERICA

INTRODUCTION

In Part One, I attempted to show what an exceptional and beneficial document our Constitution was and is. It was unique in that for perhaps the first time in history man was presented with a structure of government within which he had the opportunity to enjoy those rights our Creator bestowed upon him. But after a good and successful start, America had looked at it much too narrowly, had an incomplete understanding and appreciation of it, and had widely departed from it.

Part Two exposed many of the unfortunate things that have happened because we have ignored the Constitution and have not lived by it. To begin with, although everybody is trying mightily to acquire as much wealth as possible and has looked to the government to assist them they have not been successful. Our people really do not understand what wealth is and consequently are diverted in their quest for it, and the politicians have not helped in the process. A self-defeating system, it has resulted not in an expansion of everything the people want but a complete denial of it! The people in their mistaken philosophy believe they are working for the better good but are producing the opposite. This results because they do not understand the basic truth that lies behind the Constitution – and that is when a man works for his own personal good he is not narrowly selfish but is actually working for the good of all. Therein is the false and deadly sin of the socialistic state which inevitably results in dysfunction, undermining the right to life, liberty and the pursuit of happiness guaranteed by the Declaration of Independence.

As stated, our people do not understand wealth, and in the wrong path they have been following they have produced an economy, both in the private and public sectors, that is the opposite of what they wanted. The first evidence of this is the undeniable fact that this country is out of balance, and with this condition comes gross social inequality. Our leaders (and some economists), lacking respect for the Constitution, wish to ramp up the role of government in human affairs without grasping where this likely is to lead. In this illusion that there are no negative consequences, principles are swept down the Potomac to the open sea.

CHAPTER FIFTEEN

THE SERIOUS SHORTCOMINGS OF SOCIALISTIC STATISM AND ITS STAGNATION OF OUR ECONOMY

Introduction:

I make this opening observation. These writings on the subject of economics, I am sure, try to be objective but the personal always creeps in. In my attempts being a nonagenarian and having keenly viewed the long sweep of history over the last century, I do not deny some personal bias but also allege that historical perceptive gives it added legitimacy. I present this as a treatise on economics as an art and science with the objectivity thereof but in the writing without apology I cannot resist some personal notes which may add relevance.

This wraps up several years of my wrathful writing covering the 2008 presidential campaign during which an attempt was made to put the candidates (and some congressmen and our country) on the right path. Continuing my efforts, I sent Barack Obama a Christmas letter in 2009 telling him how to right a wrong course. I followed that by letters to the Secretary of the Treasury and the Chairman of the Federal Reserve System. There were few acknowledgments—a curt note from the White House and a short note from the Fed, pointing out my ideas would require a change in the law. I was pleased to know that the Fed was aware that there was a law.

The growth of socialistic thinking:

For a timely summary of the nature of socialism and its cast of characters, I am indebted principally to the December 31, 2009 issue of *National Review.*

Few of us have ever met someone who forthrightly admitted he was a socialist. In my long life I can recall only two – and that was decades ago.

In the first case, while waiting tables at the Yale Faculty Club in 1935, I served Norman Thomas, the perpetual socialist candidate for the presidency. Also a fellow graduate student in economics and an Oxford graduate openly admitted that he was a communist. We did not take him seriously.

In the second case, circa 1970, I recall listening to the Paris editor of *Le Monde* speak at a luncheon in New York as a guest of the Washington editor of *The New York* Times. He was reporting that the socialists had just swept into power in France. How did that happen? I offered a most inappropriate example. I reminded them of the classical recipe for cooking frogs' legs: First, you immerse the frogs in lukewarm water. The frogs are unaware of the gradual increase in heat until it is too late – the frogs are thoroughly cooked and unable to escape. They die. After the lunch, a Francophile chided me for using the word "frogs." He thought my play on words wasn't funny. I chuckled, but did not apologize. I didn't want to live in an economy slowly "cooked" to death by socialism.

The cast of American characters and their thinking:

The cited *National Review* article contained a rather complete review of the American philosophers of progressivism covering the last 130 years.

One prominent influence source was Richard Ely (1854-1943). An economics professor at Johns-Hopkins and Wisconsin, Ely was one of the pioneers of American progressivism, influenced by European thought. He had a profound effect not only on economics – he was one of the founders of the American Economics Association – but also on prominent political leaders such as Theodore Roosevelt, Woodrow Wilson and Robert LaFollette.

essentially unchanged and is universal. Yes, man's needs are implicit in human nature which changes very little over time. And basic here are two convictions set forth dramatically in the Declaration of Independence and cemented down by the Constitution: All men are created equal and no man should be governed by another without his consent. This is the bedrock upon which our economic activities are anchored or should be if we are to enjoy liberty in our daily lives as envisaged by our Founders.

Herbert Croly (1869-1930), one of the chief founders of The New Republic magazine, was an unabashed advocate of centralizing political authority as a way of achieving needed reforms. A self-proclaimed Hamiltonian, not a Jeffersonian, he rejected classical liberalism in favor of the sorts of late 19th-century reforms instituted by Otto Bismarck in the German state. Croly believed that our states would dissolve into a federal authority, which in turn would organize the economy into union-like associations of businessmen, farmers and laborers. While not really a socialist, his ideas helped pave the way for the real thing.

These were hardly the only critics of free enterprise. These critics were not very forgiving of human error or of the ability of existing institutions to correct them without indulging in grand, centrally guided social transformations. They may have read Adam Smith, but failed to grasp his points. Yet the Great Depression caused widespread dissatisfaction with capitalism. And since capitalism caused the Depression, less capitalism was the way to work our way out of it. The publication of John Maynard Keynes' *General Theory* in 1936 contributed to this rejection. I remember buying an early copy of the book at the Yale Book Store.

An unstable monetary system aids the socialists:

Our Constitution gave the Federal government authority, though not sole authority, over coinage and currency. Our citizens have a right to expect that it would do so in good faith, maintaining a stable value when used as the medium of exchange. But throughout most of our history it has given us instead built-in inflation. The creation of the Federal Reserve System did not resolve the problem. In fact, it did the opposite. Today, annual inflation is 3 percent the public accepts it, forgetting compounding and other effects. Among those are the income tax consequences when the inflated values are reflected in market-place exchanges the appreciation is considered income and is taxed.

Socialism in the twentieth century and beyond:

The damage of socialism in Europe, before and after World War II, is well-known. Yet it did not end with the dismantling of the Soviet Union and its client "Iron Curtain" states. The current situation is described by ex-Soviet dissident Vladimir Bukovsky. The European Union, in effect for more than 20 years, currently is presided over by faceless bureaucrats, the European Parliament, some 1,200 to 1,400 people, constantly traveling between moving headquarters of Brussels, Luxembourg, and Strasbourg. Bukovsky observes: "The European Union itself is becoming more and more bizarre. Each community that joins is asked to adopt 80,000 pages of regulations and rules." These are well-larded with pork – in some cases, literally. One directive requires all the owners of pig farms to supply their pigs with colored balls in case they become bored." Russian President Vladimir Putin would smile such nonsense, but right now he has other troubles.

The socialists cannot handcuff Adam Smith. Although his hand is "invisible," it votes every day through market transactions. The actions of the free market are democratic. Each sale and purchase effectively counts as a "vote." It is a superior way of arriving at the worth of things more than the assessments by elites.

Summary and conclusion:

We must bring back free markets. That means removing the government monopoly over money and banking, privatizing Social Security, Medicare and other "entitlement" programs, and ultimately, mounting a powerful case against socialism. When I speak like this to fairly intelligent people, they say, "Never! Impossible! Dreamer!" They say I am too idealistic. At least I have the right ideals, the kind rooted in human nature. Man is as materialistic as ever. Free markets are the best way of accommodating this reality.

CHAPTER SIXTEEN

OUR "MONSTEROUS" BANKING MONOPOLY

It is devastating, but is it constitutional?

This chapter owes a debt to Professor Allan Meltzer of Carnegie Mellon University, perhaps this country's leading monetary economist for the past thirty years. In his letter to me of October 30, 2009, he wrote:

> I would welcome an end to the government monopoly in banking, Years ago I discussed this issue with Professor (Friedrich) Hayek. He recognized, as I do, that the most one could hope for would be that the private banking system would exist side-by-side with the government chartered banks. He recognized, as I do, that we are unlikely to see an end to the government monopoly.

Professor Meltzer's letter was in response to my sending him a paper in which I had outlined a system for ending the government monopoly over our currency. Since receiving Professor Meltzer's letter, I have been engaged in outlining a system to privatize banking. This paper is a supplement to that effort, making clear the recurring chronic failure in it and the devastation that has caused. What has been the history, scope, character of this devastation? What can be done about it?

Our national banking system is a vast government-run monopoly with devastating effects not only on the individual but also on the entire economy. The government, rather than protecting our commercial rights to choose, has deprived us of this freedom, and without due process. This chapter, in short, is an indictment of our national banking system and how government monopoly is at the heart of it. It is also to raise serious questions of legality and violation of the Constitution.

History

Our Founders, it appears, were more adept in the art of government than they were in finance, but this may have been due to their commendable concern about taxation. This fledgling government had financial problems from the start and had difficulties coping with them. This is very well described in Harlow Giles Unger's "The Last Founding Father: James Monroe and a Nation's Call to Greatness." On page 213, the author notes: (quote from page)

Then there was a depression in 1819. It did not last long, but it had serious repercussions. Congress, reluctantly, passed some laws. Unger states (p. 296):

> Early in 1819, however, the nation's first financial
> panic introduced some decidedly ill feeling into
> the Era of Good Feelings. Inflated by speculation
> in western lands, an economic "bubble" suddenly
> popped with hundreds of banks shutting down,
> and thousands of depositors and investors wiped
> out. The land rush had seen the number of banks
> grow to more than 1,000, with each issuing its own

colorful bank notes—normally in two-and five-dollar denominations backed by no one knew what. One Rhode Island bank with capitalization of only $145 issued bank notes with a total face value of $800,000. Borrowers nonetheless scooped them up, along with millions of similar notes from other banks to buy federal lands in the wilderness at $2.00 an acre—sight unseen. All hoped to repay their loans with earning from the land. With money to be made, speculators rushed into the mix, borrowing banknotes as fast as banks could print them and buying land to resell to gullible settlers who never checked whether the speculators actually owned the lands they sold or sold the same lands multiple times. Concerned over runaway speculation and fraudulent land sales, Congress passed a law requiring banks to back the paper they issued with specie—coins, gold, silver, and so forth. As the first few insolvent banks closed their door, depositors staged a run on the rest, and forced them to try to call in loans or shut their doors. Most of them shut their doors.

Without any laws on the books to deal with the panic, the president was helpless. The Constitution had left control over banking to the states, and few members of the Republican-controlled Congress were willing to tolerate extension of federal powers into yet another industry. Using the only economic weapon in it hands, Congress raised tariffs to protect American goods from overseas competition and force American merchants and consumers to spend more money at home.

In the 19th century amazing and unprecedented growth took place in this country, both geographically and economically. It is not surprising that imperfections and problems should arise in financial and other matters. These, however, did not slow the growth. Free-market capitalism prevailed fairly well throughout all of this economic growth but it was blamed for most of these problems. Amidst all of this a revolution in social thinking and consciousness sprung up. Slaves were freed after a bloody war, which also strengthened the Federal powers. In the latter part of the century, radical and liberal thinkers began to emerge with Marx and Engels and perhaps encouraging the likes of Richard Ely, John Dewey and Herbert Croly among economists and Oliver Wendell Holms, Jr. among jurists.

Industrial bigness and the rapid growth of corporations, compounded by consolidations, mergers and acquisitions, were fertile subjects upon which these critics pounced. Much of this was fully justified in view of the abuses and greed that had accompanied this rapid, out-of-control growth. The emergence of large financial institutions to fund and finance all this growth also brought with it its own excesses and abuses, which did not escape the critics. Robber barons had emerged. And Theodore Roosevelt and other politicians became gladiators to confront these barons.

At the start of the 20th century anti-trust, anti-monopoly and other legislation was enacted to eliminate unfair restraints of trade, attempting to bring back free and wholesome competition. But after some fumbling some significant gains were achieved (Big Oil and Big Telephone were broken up.) After WWII this country almost completely forgot about these laws. Bigness was encouraged and the badness it brought with it was overlooked by both Federal and state governments, supporting special interest in the process. With the Chrysler crisis in 1979, we even adopted a credo, "too big to fail," having overlooked the fact that our laws and regulators should have kept businesses from becoming too big to exist.

Our National banking monopoly

In our daily business and commercial lives we have three major needs: (1) a need for a medium of exchange; (2) a need for a safe and profitable place to put our savings; and (3) a need for credit, reasonably-priced, to supply the capital we need where we do not have the liquid resources. The Constitution does not say anywhere that the federal government has the right to a monopoly in satisfying these needs. Yet in spite of this, the government has gradually has monopolized our currency, banking and credit. What's more, it decides who should get such credit and the terms thereof.

Many people are mystified over any suggestion that the current monetary system constitutes a monopoly. Surely, they note, there are thousands of banks and others providing these services in this country in apparent competition with each other. "How can you call this a monopoly?" they ask. I respond this way: Monopoly is not simply a matter of ownership. It ultimately is about *control*. These institutions, formally speaking, are in the private sector. Yet they operate under a form of government control that is far-ranging in operations. To the naked eye, these operations may be invisible. But they are real all the same. Under antitrust law, they would be illegal. Yet the government doesn't necessarily live by laws it sets for everyone else. And it pushes for further control as time progresses.

Government intervention in the petroleum industry provides an apt comparison. Typically, the large oil companies own or franchise a number of service stations many in one marketing area. What choice does the consumer have? Only what station he uses. Further, oil prices are set at the margin by OPEC, the oil monopoly, and so the gasoline prices are largely set by that monopoly. And our government here, rather than fighting that monopoly (they could have set up and "OPIC", an organization of petroleum importing countries), has helped support OPEC, even giving it military support at times.

Petroleum is another super-monopoly that all of have accepted, feeling helpless. But we are only blind; we are far from helpless. This country had adequate natural resources, skills and capital to make this country petroleum self-sufficient if it would only operate in the common-sense, free-market mode.

We are completely "conned" into accepting these vast, invisible monopolies in oil and banking. We even applaud the government's actions. When many small or unbailed-out banks are closed, the FDIC (part of the government's monopoly) saves most of the depositors, but management and shareholders (and others) suffer. Most of these failures have been caused by the unfair competition that the monopoly has waged against them including subsidizing lower interest rates and availability of capital to the monopoly members. And these foreclosed banks will then have a big struggle to reorganize and again serve their customers. This is a very visible part of the devastation caused by this national banking monopoly.

Many writers waste much time in a detailed examination of the decade of the 1930s looking for causes and solutions. All history teaches us is that all we can learn from history is our innocence and intellectual inadequacies.

Our perceptions of this pachyderm, product of our Federal government, is no more acute or better than that of blind men (per the classic story) making meticulous examination of all of the elephant's parts but ending up with no comprehension or understanding of what an elephant really looks like or is. Not always is it easier to see things when they are big. It took mankind a very, very long time to see that the world is round. That is why we cannot see or comprehend the monolithic monster that is our national banking system. The only sources of the resources which provide the credit capital are found in producing more than we are consuming, giving us no only what we need now, but also providing the need for future growth in the capitalistic mode. Our government cannot manufacture any of this but it can misdirect the flows so we end up the poorer, not the richer. The wheels may spin fast but they go no place.

Almost all institutions engaged in banking and banking-related services in the United States are chartered, controlled, regulated and, in effect, sponsored by the Federal government. This control is reinforced by the Comptroller of the Currency who gives outright help to national banks. Our central bank, the Federal Reserve System, also augments this centralization of powers, facilitating interbank lending and discounting their securities backed by the full-faith and credit of the government, to promote liquidity and relieving the banks from their responsibility for maintaining a sound fractional-reserve system. This is not to mention the subsidized interest rates set at rates well below those of international credit markets. These banks are permitted to form holding companies and engage in many types of business. Recently, any financial institution could be designated a bank whenever the Fed decided to call it one.

The monopoly described above has been further empowered by concentrations of banks ("mega-banks"), principally on Wall Street, whose functions include brokerage and underwriting on a massive national scale. When their reckless credit practices, driven by greed, got this country into a liquidity crisis, the Federal government jumped in with great infusions of credit and printing-press money to help this giant group which had become "too big to fail." Such actions were justified by claiming they were needed to avoid a complete meltdown. Congress is now making a show of investigating all of this, forgetting to bring a mirror to the hearings. And so far Washington has not seen the errors of its ways and is on course to repeat its past errors.

Goldman Sachs mines no gold, but they are the wily quarterback that directs the game and they seldom get "sacked." I shall not list here other major players, but they are well-known as members of this special Club. Not only does Goldman Sachs play quarterback, but it provides much of the management talent for leaders at the Department of the Treasury and other federal agencies. The top executives at Goldman Sachs can rightfully be considered as being interns in training for these top Washington jobs!

Many within these mega-banks, etc. feel they are in competition with each other, but this is all intra-mural. What one loses, another may gain, but in the end the taxpayers lose. It is not even a zero-sum game. But where they compete with what remains of the private banking industry the latter does not have a chance. No wonder there have been so many failures, with many more in prospect. Certainly, nobody today would consider starting a private bank without the blessing of those in control.

This indictment of our national banking system would be incomplete without mentioning our securities exchanges. As a most important ancillary of our banking system, facilitating the raising and free flow of capital funds, they also deserve to be indicted.

The free and open exchange of securities under the buttonwood tree on lower Manhattan has completely disappeared, and securities trading has degenerated into a money-grubbing, greedy monopoly like banking has. The stock exchanges, particularly the New York Stock Exchange, should have their own self-regulating, non-profit organization owned by the listed members and charged with the responsibility of maintaining orderly markets, with free and active competition and transparency at all times. This has completely disappeared. The stock exchanges themselves have become listed, profit-directed corporations, operating solely in the interest of their shareholders. The excuse perhaps is that this regulatory function is performed by the SEC. But the SEC has never had the resources or the competence to even begin to do that, as recent events have clearly shown. Washington is too close to the politicians and too far from Wall Street.

Like our banking system, this adjunct to the banking system has become a monopoly, part of the great monopoly. Here, too, we have had a betrayal of public trust by our leaders.

Is this banking monopoly and control over commerce constitutional?

The preamble to the Constitution says it was to promote "the general Welfare". Unfortunately, our national banking system has not done that; in fact, it has put many people on welfare.

Article I, Section 8. "The Congress shall have Power... To borrow money on the credit of the United States... To regulate Commerce with foreign Nations, and among the several States, and with the Indian Tribes,... To Coin Money, regulate Value thereof, and of foreign Coins...."

Amendment IX. The enumeration in the Constitution of certain rights shall not be construed to deny or disparage others retained by the people.

Amendment X. The powers not delegated to the United States by the Constitution, nor prohibited by it to the States, are reserved to the States respectively, or to the people.

From the above, we must conclude the following:

> The power to coin money was not given exclusively to government, but could be exercised by the people, i.e. it could be privatized.

> Where government borrows money, it must be on its own credit. This says nothing about the people borrowing money; that is a private, contractual matter.

> When it ways that the government shall have the power to regulate commerce with foreign nations, among the several states and with the Indian tribes, it certainly did not mean the *direct action* of government with these entities. It is clear from history and the clear intent of our Founders that when they said "to control", they meant (using the language of the times) "to make regular." "to make proper." Our Founders and their countrymen were actively engaged in commerce, in many businesses, in running plantations and farming, and in international trade of their products for the industrial goods they could not manufacture. They wished to encourage free trade in all of this. The reason this was inserted was because during the Confederacy, some states had enacted laws prohibiting citizens of adjoining states from entering into commerce in their state, and they wanted to prohibit that absolutely,

so as noted, using the language of the times, they said "to regulate," meaning "to make proper and regular."

Unfortunately, when the Supreme Court first faced up to the question of whether government could really control commerce, they missed the proper meaning completely, and as subsequent Courts have not reversed this, there has been a completely false acceptance that government can control commerce. That is the antithesis of the free trade our Constitution mandates.

CHAPTER SEVENTEEN

COMPLAINTS TO THE PRESS

A Fair Explanation of "Fair Share."

Published in the Johnston, Pa. *Tribune-Democrat* in
September 2011.

Writer offered lesson in basic, economics

The Sept. 6 letter, "Everyone deserves a fair share," is lacking in substance and basic economics.

"How many rich Wal-Mart workers do you know?" the writer asks. Wal-Mart workers who earn their keep really keep all people from getting poorer by helping supply their needs at a fair price.

The writer says there is only so much money, showing she wrongly, equates money with wealth. Our fiat money has no value except in expediting exchange transactions in all markets.

President Obama has made the same mistake; he has produced all kinds of money in large quantities, but has produced no wealth, no jobs.

An employer, to stay in business, can put money in the hands of his employees to the extent they have added that much value to his end product. When he does that, the worker in spending that money makes jobs for other workers. But if he can only put less money into the hands of the workers because of taxes and regulatory expenses that must be withheld, the result is that in the spending process other workers receive less and cannot produce equivalent values.

Wealth (and jobs) can be created only by entrepreneurs, big and small, who are willing to risk their resources, plus those they must borrow when they have confidence there is a fair chance they can operate without having the government throwing sprags into the wheels of their operations.

The writer concludes: "Everyone deserves a fair share of the pie."

Those who think like her should spend more time in worrying about the size of the pie, not their piece of it.

GEORGE J. HEIDEMAN
TEQUESTA, FLA., FORMERLY OF LIGONIER

Socialism Failed in 1620. It Will Fail in 2020.
(not published)

November 28, 2011

To the Editor:

The 99-percenters protesting have failed in many subjects--history, economics and mathematics. They are complaining about fractions, not equality. It would be simple to give them equality at 100 percent, and that would be to take all the wealth from the one-percenters and distribute it to the 99-percenters. Thus they would have 100 percent equality, but at near-poverty level. But this would force them to consume all of the wealth, leaving no seed for planting the crop in the next year! That is what they are really calling for but they do not realize it.

The change the protesters are calling for should be to a system of equal opportunity that our Founders established and had served us exceptionally well for so many years. It appears, however, they want to go to a faulty system where opportunity is denied the individual. This might give us equality but at a very low level. Although this country is already well along on this road to socialism, the protesters don't realize it is that about which they should be protesting. They are complaining about getting a small piece of the pie, forgetting that it is the size of the pie that is important. Our history before: we had big government clearly showed how to increase the size of the pie and in the process people got larger pieces.

Let us go back much farther in history, to 1620, when the Pilgrims established Plymouth Plantation. It was a communal venture with common property that all were asked to work. Only with the help of friendly Indians who gave them corn and showed them how to plant it were they able to survive the first two years, and over half of them did not make it. But in 1623, led by Governor Bradford, they chose to replace the collective farming they had been practicing and assigned every family its own parcel of land. Governor Bradford noted the amazing results: "This had very good success, for it made all hands very industrious, so much more corn was planted than otherwise would have been." Crops became much larger and better. As they were freed from economic communism and entered into individual enterprise abundance began to come upon them.

It is clear that we must change our flawed system that is constantly getting worse. We must reduce the size and heavy hand of big government from our daily lives, and let the people plant their own corn on their own land. Industriousness and prosperity will return with the opportunities that only a free-market system can provide. Then we can have abundance without the help of 'friendly Indians' from China and other countries.

OUR CONFUSED ECONOMISTS. Exhibit A. Paul Krugman, Nobel Winner.

September 2011
To the *Palm Beach Post*, September 2011. Published.

Krugman hairbrained about government's role.

This is a commentary upon Paul Krugman's "Setting their hair on fire" column last Sunday. The only thing consistent about Krugman is his shallowness and stupidity which his column shows. His hair is not on fire, but he is hairbrained.

Writing about President Obama's "Jobs Act" comedy last Thursday, Mr. Krugman says he was "favorably impressed", but didn't think the plan was as bold as Mr. Krugman would have liked it to be. Krugman concluded that if the jobs bill becomes law, "it would probably make a significant dent in unemployment." If he had really deserved the Nobel Prize in Economics, he would have been more definite and positive than that, and would have been in strong opposition to any bill of that kind.

The balance of his column was equally devoid of substance deserving of any notice except for his evaluation of the Federal Reserve System. He set it right that the stated purpose of that System was to keep price levels stable and to promote employment. Although a failure in this now and in the most years since the "Fed" was established, he still tries to defend it.

Mr. Krugman is still looking for the hand of big government to bring magic in monetary and fiscal policy to create jobs. The only way to create jobs is to give the private sector the ability to do so and not expect the heavy hand of government to do so.

George J. Heideman

DON'T WORRY ABOUT THE ENTITLEMENTS.
THEY RE PREPAID.
(Letters to the Editor. The *Palm Beach Post*. February 2012.)

In the referenced letter, the writer said: "It is annoying to continually hear Social Security and Medicare referred to as 'entitlements'. When politicians, mostly from the right, talk about cutting "entitlements', it sounds much more reasonable than if they said they want to cut everyone's "prepaid benefits.' While I realize that The Post cannot control how complainers talk, the paper should make an honest effort to use the right terminology." But The Post did little to set matters straight when it headlined the article "Entitlements are prepaid." That is why I was very pleased when it printed my strong complaint.

Those 'prepaid' entitlement funds never were invested

The writer of the letter, "Entitlements are prepaid," uses reasoning comparable to those "investors' in other Ponzi schemes who thought they were safe because they had prepaid.

The obvious basic flaw is that these prepayments were not invested. And that is the basic reason why nobody would believe they will be receiving these promised entitlement benefits.

Yes, all of us thought that these billions we and our employers were prepaying would be invested, but they were not. They were spent by our Ponzi politicians on pumping up government, so now we have big government, big debts, big deficits and perhaps big defaults, but we do not have the big funds we thought we would have. Those "prepayments" have become pittances, and we are now being offered more of this Ponzification.

GEORGE J. HEIDEMAN
Tequesta

FRANK REID COMPLAINS LOUDLY ABOUT

OUTSOURCING U.S. OLYMPIC UNIFORMS TO CHINA.

July 31, 2012

Chinese did a nice job on Olympic uniforms.

It is hard to believe the uproar being made about "outsourcing" generally and the fact that the uniforms for the U.S. Olympic team have been beautifully and competitively made in China ("Offshoring emblematic of nation's woes," letter to the editor).

Hasn't anybody heard about free trade? How can we expect "insourcing" without "outsourcing?" International trade benefits everybody. It is a two-way street. If the U.S. would restrict trade with China, etc., and impose import tariffs, the uproar would be deafening. Besides the purpose of the Olympics is to promote international good will and good feelings. Senate Majority Leader Harry Reid, D-Nev., undoubtedly does not know that. He knows only demagoguery.

Why do companies outsource? Obviously, to stay in business and thus retain jobs here when they are faced with high labor costs here, which makes them noncompetitive in certain products and operations. It is a matter of survival and self-preservation, and patriotism has nothing to do with it. You can't meet payrolls with patriotism. And Sen. Reid and many of his legislative counterparts have been and are responsible for much of these higher labor costs.

GEORGE J. HEIDEMAN
Tequesta

THE DEFENSE OF MARRIAGE ACT DEFINED

THE ROE v. WADE DECISION WAS AN ABORTION

(not published)

October 19, 2012

To the Editor:

In your issue today you reported that several federal appeals courts had declared The Defense of Marriage Act unconstitutional because it was discriminatory. The only thing this proves is that we have some incompetent judges on the appeals courts. They do not even know contract law, and this is entirely a matter of contract law.

To begin with, the Constitution is a structure of government and most of the little law it contains was an afterthought--the Bill of Rights. But it incorporates and makes binding all the laws observed in the colonies, including English common law. And this includes the right of the people freely to contract with each other, a right confirmed by the Constitution. The Constitution does not mention "discrimination" but the only true discrimination would be if a law were passed denying any of these rights. But there have been no such violations here.

The "Defense of Marriage Act" was not a law; it merely assured that for centuries there had been valid contracts between man and woman whose civil rights and terms had been defined through the years by law and precedent, and to be valid are simply a matter of public record so that the public is on notice. This right of contract is freely available to all, including the so-called "Gays", who can enter into contracts covering the same or similar civil rights. These contracts then should be publicly recorded so the public is on notice. The courts would certainly uphold those contracts. But the fact that these contracts would have to be publicly recorded does not mean they are marriage contracts, and it would be wrong to term them so and to make them subject to the same civil rights legitimate marriage contracts entail.

The .Constitution and its antecedents assure us of equality in many things bestowed upon us by our Creator. If there is any discrimination against the "Gays", for that we must blame our Creator, and he is far remove from the jurisdiction of any appeals or other courts!

There is a greater judicial error in this area and that is the Supreme Court decision in Roe v. Wade where abortion was upheld simply on the basis of women having a right to privacy. There is no such right but in fact it is a matter of personal preference for a person to limit his natural right and wish to associate with other persons. Man is a gregarious animal always seeking and welcoming "togetherness."

Abortion is a personal, not a private matter, and it usually involves several persons, including the person within the womb.

That to deprive a person of his cherished right to associate is evident when a person may be sentenced to solitary confinement in prison. That is severe punishment.

The Supreme Court should spend more time on recognizing and enforcing those laws called for by the Constitution and not waste time by inventing new rights that have no foundation.

GEORGE J. HEIDEMAN
Tequesta, Fl.

CHAPTER EIGHTEEN

WITHOUT CONSTITUTIONAL CONFORMANCE THERE CAN BE NO ACTUAL AMERICA.

When reading I have written in the preceding chapters, many might retort "So what?." The Constitution is no longer relevant. Starting in 1933 with Franklin Roosevelt's "New Deal", the theme has been that the demands of this growing country are such that we must move on from that philosophy. This new philosophy has been pushed ever since by the major political parties. The Democrats have engraved it as what they stand for but the Republicans have not been far behind. In short, the interests and rights of the individual must be subordinated for the greater good of society!

This nation has succumbed to this although it had been warned about it happening from the start. This warning started about 2,500 years ago, with Aristotle, continued by John Locke, and prominently mentioned by James Madison. I repeat from Chapter One:

> Aristotle stated that the greatest benefactor was he
> who came up with the idea and founded the state.
> But he warned that the same man if separated from
> law and justice may become the worst since armed
> injustice is the most dangerous, and he is equipped
> from birth with the arms of intelligence and with
> moral qualities which he may use for the worst ends.

We have a Constitution based on an ordered liberty. There are two major reasons. First, if we are to have freedom and quality of life we all want. Secondly, the practical. It is the only way this country can again grow and prosper, with all people having the opportunity to share in it.

I was the recipient of a timely and solid support for the above from the libertarian Cato Institute in its "Letter" for fall 2012, in a scholarly "The Origins of State and Government" by Tom G. Palmer, who is a senior fellow of the Institute. He criticized Obama's preposterous proclamation in 2012: "If you've been successful you did not get there on your own. If you were successful someone along the line gave you some help. Somebody helped to create this unbelievable American system that we have that allowed you to thrive. Somebody invested in roads and bridges. If you've got a business--you didn't build that. Somebody else made that happen."

Palmer proceeds to point out: "It cannot be the case that all wealth is attributable to the state. Historically, the existence of a state required a surplus to sustain it in the first place," adding, "The state is, at its core, a predatory institution." And he proceeds: "Modern states also claim to be the sole source of law. But historically, states mainly replace customary law with imposed law. There is a great deal of law all around us that is not a product of the state, for law is a byproduct of voluntary interaction."

Palmer then contrasts the absolute power of the traditional sovereigns with our departure with individual power plus another kind of social order involving "customary law", acquiring force little by little and by common consent of the people themselves, often taking years. But that force is real and solid because it comes from the people, the ultimate sovereigns. But there is one provision---unless the people have reasoned and met together to accept a binding structure for that new kind of social order, we have nothing but an unstable nation, with lawyers constantly passing new laws outside of any accepted purpose or principles. And a society of individuals without such unity cannot exist, and it cannot be a sovereign nation.

Tom Palmer notes (as I have) the laws that were made valid laws by the Constitution were the pre-existing" customary laws", some written, some accepted without being written. They were accepted and followed by the colonies generally, and made up much of the body of inalienable rights carried from the Declaration to the Constitution. The Constitution cemented down and perpetuated the legality of passing laws (plus the due process to enforce them) coming from the people, enforced by the people, a people united in the United States of America.

Palmer proceeds: "The evolution of freedom has involved a long process of bringing power under law." Opposing this has been the unfortunate acceptance that imposition of force from above is a necessity before there can be any laws, a "powerful imprint on our minds". That is why the socialistic state has been so readily accepted by our innocent people.

Palmer pins all of this down, concluding:

> All of us, collectively and individually, are accessories to this great sin of all time, this real original sin, a hereditary fault that can be excised and erased only with great difficulty and slowly, by an insight into pathology, by a will to recover, by the active remorse of all. It takes work to free our minds from our dependence on the state.

When meditating on what it means to live as free people we should never forget that the state doesn't grant to us our identities or our rights. The American Declaration of Independence states, "That to secure these rights, Governments have been instituted among men." We secure what is already ours. The state can add value when it helps us to do that, but rights and society are prior to the state. It's critical to remember that the next time someone says, "You didn't build that.

PART 4

A DYSFUNCTIONAL CONSTITUTION, A DYSFUNCTIONAL AMERICA

CHAPTER NINETEEN

THE REPEAL OF THE FIRST AMENDMENT AND THE ATTEMPTS TO REPEAL THE SECOND AMENDMENT

Before discussing the repeal of amendments it is necessary to define what amendments really are. In doing this I am repeating certain truths I have attempted to set forth throughout this book. The adoption of an amendment does not make it law. The Constitution, correctly understood, is a bill of rights more basic and comprehensive than that set forth by the First Amendment, which was a vehicle through which to secure ratification. For all of the freedoms and rights of man we must go back to the Enlightenment's inalienable rights of man. But our courts, including the Supreme Court, have never recognized this, and have, improvised as they went along. Article III of the Constitution recognizers this possibility and wisely gave courts the right to rule not only using law and equity but also over "controversies," but this did not mean that man could forget principles in ruling, but that there was a solid bedrock under all of this which were the inalienable rights.

Accepting the First Amendment, there must be an understanding that it is not absolute. The freedoms must be exercised responsibly in consideration of the rights of others. In other words, rights will collide. There must be ways to resolve disputes. In exercising the freedom of speech and of the press, actions must conform to basic standards of responsibility. Certainly debate and honest discussion to be permitted but their substance, purposes and objectives must be within the bounds of responsibility. In the exercise of free speech today this is ignored by a great many people. When confronted with this basic logic and truth, they have no answer and so they claim the Constitution is out of date.

Looking at the Second Amendment we have an entirely different situation when it comes to protesting gun violence. This amendment is based on our rights to defend ourselves responsibly. Most of these protestors have never read the amendment which says: "A well-regulated Militia, being necessary to the security of a free state, the right of the people to keep and bear arms shall not be infringed." Thus any attempts to restrict the proper use of firearms would be in direct conflict with the proper purpose of this amendment. Any attempt to write a bill listing all of the circumstances where firearms could be used responsibly would be impossible because they are almost infinite. This is a matter that only the judiciary can determine.

But there is a Constitutional way and basis to support proper legislation here. This appears in Article 1, Section 9 of the Constitution which states: "The writ of Habeas Corpus shall not be suspended unless when in cases of Rebellion or Insurrection the public safety requires it."

Although the federal government has taken away many of our freedoms, any further encroachment might well amount to a suspension of the writ of habeas corpus. But the violent protests of the many anti-gun people have provided the ammunition here to attack. With many statistics, they might have a solid basis to show that the public safety requires extraordinary, emergency action.

An act should be passed for the purpose of improving public safety that any person threatened by gun violence or any person witnessing such a threat has a right to present a complaint to the court for the alleged perpetrator to appear in court. Should he fail to appear or if he appears and claims there is no reasonable cause and due process has not been followed, then the court can suspend his writ of habeas corpus and order him legally to appear. The court then can follow all reasonable procedures to determine whether or not the defendant is the kind of person that might be capable of unreasonable and improper gun violence, using expert witnesses such as psychologists. If the court then decides there is a reasonable probability that the defendant could endanger the public safety, then it could order the defendant to turn over all firearms to the court. The court might also require the defendant to post bond guaranteeing further compliance. Should there be further infractions, the bond funds would be turned over to the court, and with further infractions the defendant could be fined and finally jailed.

It is, of course, up to the Congress to decide whether there is really an emergency here that the public safety requires extraordinary action. I do not know if today there is much more gun violence than in our past history, or if the severity of it now warrants this unusual action. There would appear to be reasonable cause however for them to take appropriate actions.

With a legal and reasonable law on the books, the politicians would no longer have any foundation for calling for action. Any protests here could be answered by a simple suggestion, to look at the law. What more can possibly be legally done?

CHAPTER TWENTY

THE POISON OF EXCESSIVE PARTISANSHIP AND ITS CONSTITUTIONAL ANTIDOTE

In the Cato Policy Report of January/February 2012 appeared a very interesting and provocative article, "James Madison and the Origins of Partisanship." This article discussed "the benefits and burdens of partisanship" and places it within its interesting historical context.

This article was centered on a recent book, "James Madison Rules America: The Constitutional Origins of Congressional Partisanship" by William F. Connelly, Jr., the John K. Boardman Professor of Politics at Washington and Lee University. The author views Congress as the "broken branch of government." I contend that it isn't just Congress but the executive and judicial branches that are broken. Our major parties represent many contending groups and interests and the heated interplay does little other than corrupt our politics. The checks and balances built into our Constitution now seem unable to operate and we are faced with confounding confrontations. We appear to be stuck on dead center.

James Madison was right when he observed "No free country has ever been without parties, which are a natural offspring of freedom." We might not agree with author Connelly when he concludes "partisanship is rooted in the Constitution," but I strongly disagree with him when he contends "the Constitution governs parties more than the parties govern the Constitution."

Connelly observes that partisanship is both good and bad. The bad we see every day. It is not only the way the party in power exploits its power over all branches of government but also the way it exploits government when not in office, in refusing to compromise. This prevents us from attaining the objectives in the preamble to our Constitution, which include "To form a more perfect union... insure domestic tranquility... promote the general welfare." That is why we are "stuck on dead center." This country is caught in a Constitutional contradiction of its own making.

Connelly rightly cites a number of causes for heightened partisanship including: party primaries, especially in congressional elections; gerrymandered redistricting; institutional reforms such as those in the 1970s designed to make Congress more open and democratic; growth of government; the overuse of regulation; and the concentration of major media. Connelly adds: "... The growth of government and the concomitant increased stake in our politics contribute to increased partisan polarization. Big government gives you big politics." Today, politics is about everything and everything is about politics.

All too many newspapers are inject partisanship into the news. Also, the "accident" where there might have been competitive newspapers but one prevailed resulted in that community becoming partisan. But not only the economic success of the newspapers but also all other areas of expanding media became affected in this same way. They have each in their own way affected the depth and direction of this extreme partisanship. In this environment it has become impossible not only for a bit of moderation, but also any evaluation of issues and principles on their merits. It is no wonder that the Constitution has become an *obiter dicta*.

Connelly also correctly observes that "the dramatic increase in education among Americans augments polarization. One of the first things parents look for when choosing a college for their children is the "color" of its political leaning; I know of no colleges or universities that can rightly be called even "moderate." And this polarization also flows over into the field of religion.

But, as previously stated, I thoroughly disagree with Connelly's conclusion: "The most fundamental cause of partisan polarization may be our 200-year old constitutional system which invites the spirit of party in our politics." To the contrary and as set forth herein, any such spirit is minimal and the complete thrust of the Constitution properly read and interpreted is contrary to having a government run by parties where the individual is submerged to the group. The Constitution mandates a government of the people, by the people, and for the people, not one of parties.

It seems the correct summary of the problem and conundrum set forth above to note that it boils down to a direct conflict between power and principles, a never-ending conflict imbued in our human nature, which was acknowledged by James Madison as had Aristotle many centuries before him. W. Lee Rawls points out in his commentary on Connelly's book: "Madison would not be on the sidelines about purported fouls in legislative process. He would be in the middle of it, moving ahead rapidly maximizing whatever he thought was the best policy. For Madison, you can choose bipartisanship, or you can go your merry partisan way. You can seek a policy outcome, or seek political advantage."

Rawls concludes his article by referring to his own book on the legislative system, "In Praise of Deadlock: How Partisan Struggle Makes Better Laws": "Advocates of post-partisanship politics invoke a new era in which these tensions dissolve... the existent legislative machine will not grant them their wishes." He then adds that "as long as political parties remain the unit of cooperation within the American political system, and it is difficult to imagine American democracy without them, then desire of the post-partisans... will remain unfulfilled." He adds another point with which, as before, I am in complete agreement: "In short, all Americans should feel that they can enter the political fray, love their country, and fight hard; and certainly don't let anybody tell you that they have all of the answers."

This is my part in the fray. I am completely for bipartisanship. I contend further that the complete Constitution permits and requires that principles must prevail over power. Accordingly, if we are to conform our present government to the Constitution, we must take those strong actions to outlaw the excessive partisanship that pervades this country, and take the stronger steps that are necessary to get us firmly back on the right constitutional course.

In my view had our Founding Fathers in writing of the Constitution even remotely contemplated and envisioned this sorry state of affairs they would have put something in that document to prevent it. This exercise of raw power is perhaps not unconstitutional (although the preamble disavowed such forces) but it certainly is extra-Constitutional and therefore in that area of governance that the Constitution can properly and legitimately address.

It is not too late. We should declare major political parties illegal at the Federal level. Parties would be permitted to operate at the sub-Federal level, freely within the States and subject to their jurisdiction. The right to run or join political parties is not a right guaranteed by the Constitution.

As a consistent part of this radical reform movement, the incoming president before taking the oath of office would be required to disaffiliate and resign from all political parties, thus making it clear that he was committed to act in the best interests of the entire country. Clearly being publicly committed to fulfilling his oath of office, the Constitution would be uppermost in his mind. Further, at the end of his term should he choose to run for re-election, he would automatically be on the ballot with no political affiliation indicated. Further, members of the House of Representatives should have four-year rather than two-year terms. Under the present system, partisanship is promoted. The moment a representative gets seated, he feels he must start running for re-election, with his party organization being uppermost in his mind.

To conform to the Constitution, there is a further major change required, and it has much indeed in its favor. This is the redistricting process which takes place every ten years. The present system is very disruptive and disorderly, and represents partisanship at its worst. It is now in the hands of the legislature in each state, and they fight bitterly over it, frequently calling for judicial help to settle the matter. But the major objection is that it is unconstitutional.

Since 1790, Congress has applied five different methods of apportioning representation among the states. Finally, in 1929, being unable to make a reapportionment after the census of 1920, Congress decided to cap the number of Representatives at 435, the present number now. With the growing and shifting population, each state's number of Representatives usually is changing, thus requiring setting up geographically new districts to elect each. This conflict is entirely out of keeping with the essence of the Constitution which mandates free and equal people reasoning together in the political process to arrive at peaceful and practical resolutions of their differences. And this is the basic fault here.

To back off a bit, in kingdoms the power and authority to rule was in the king, the sovereign. In the United States this sovereignty is clearly in the people, and the people in the Constitution have distributed their sovereignty as per the Bill of Rights, Amendment X, with the states insisting that this be made clear. This Amendment is short and concise; "The power not delegated to the United States by the Constitution nor prohibited by it to the States, are reserved to the States respectively, or to the people."

Thus, the election of the people to rule over them is a direct action of each person, and cannot be delegated, but here it has been delegated to the state legislatures, thus creating an unsupported and illegal sub-sovereign area. The election of representatives in all of its aspects must remain with the people, and that requires a fixed formula, not subject to political manipulation.

This solution can be very simple, forthright and direct. I am proposing what might be called the "ABCD System", where the alphabetical listing of people in the census is broken down into the number of groups equal to the authorized number of Representatives, and then each alphabetical group will elect one Representative, thus assuring state-wide representation of the people of the state, their proper function. An alternative might be a fixed, geographical formula, dividing the state by north-south or east-west straight lines adjusted to capture the designated population.

Obviously, this Constitutional change would have many benefits, being more efficient, less costly, less partisan, elimination of grotesque gerrymandering, reduction in "earmarking", and eliminating most situations where the same representative was constantly re-elected from "his own" district, loved by the people for the "goodies" he promises and brings to them.

These changes would give states more autonomy. In place of two major parties there might very well emerge several "independent" parties. In the naming and selection of candidates, there would still be primaries, and each party would select its own candidates for local, state and national offices, including Senators and President. They then most likely would have party conventions to narrow the final choices.

With diluted power, more principled laws would be passed. The milk of our country-wide politics would then be more likely to produce cream rather than sour milk. Thankfully, the millions of thinking people of this country are aware of and seriously concerned about the catastrophe that awaits us unless drastic changes are soon made. These are times that bring forth many constructive ideas. Coincidentally, in the *National Review* issue of February 21, 2011, appeared an article by William Vogeli "The Sense of the Senate" commencing "One thing leads to another. Complain bitterly that the Senate filibusters undermine democracy and you wind up concluding that the Senate's existence is undemocratic." Vogeli, however proceeds to point out that the Senate is really necessary to make our government truly democratic. In support of this he refers also to Madison's rationale and justification for having a Senate. These are more pertinent today than even prior to 1913 when the Seventeenth Amendment authorized the election of senators by the people of each state rather than their legislators.

This article observes using Madison's "conundrum" (power vs. principle) and the thoughts of others that liberty may well be endangered by the abuses of liberty as well as by the abuses of power. Further we should not accept that government is automatically good by being democratic, the acceptance of which will make us complacent about what out democracy actually does. "The disease most incident to popular government" is what Madison calls the "majority faction." In Federalist 63 he argued that an institution like the Senate at some constitutional distance from the people" may be sometimes necessary as a defense for the people against their own temporary errors and delusions." The goal always, is for "the cool and deliberate sense of community."

This "cool and deliberate sense of the community" operates constantly and accounts for changes in the majority party. The 2010 congressional elections are a good example. One might argue that the Tea Party represented a "sense of the community." Democracy allows for self-correction. Our bicameral government provides some balance and breathing space against pure democracy and the better democracy for which we should always strive.

Vogeli points out that the 1913 Amendment brought the Senate closer to the people and "had the unintended consequence of re-affirming the distinct role of the States, as such, in discharging governmental responsibilities and engaging the people in self-government." Our big and expanding Federal government is clear evidence that it has taken on excessive powers, minimizing the powers of the States and thus the power of the people. This is democracy disintegrating and needs to be stopped. We need a new Federalism. The time is ripe for this now, with plurality of governors elected now who favor limiting the powers of the Federal government.

CHAPTER TWENTY-ONE

THE GOSPEL AND THE 2012 ELECTION

Many people say that politics and religion cannot mix. Yet they can be sees as components of the same foundation of our country. Our government was established to preserve the unalienable rights given us by our Creator, some of which are enumerated in the first ten amendments to our Constitution (the Bill of Rights.) That government was limited to doing only what was necessary to protect these rights and our freedom to exercise them. These "inalienable rights" are internalized and completely contained in the religions which we practice. And our freedom to exercise religion was positively set forth in the first of the Bill of Rights amendments.

In the 2012 election campaign, we saw this fixed and inescapable combination of politics and religion. But in our internal, constitutional exercise of our religion, we have seen in essence a complete denial of this freedom! The churches in ministering to their members have been prohibited from talking about politics! If they do so, their economic existence is jeopardized by the threatened non-deductibility of their support from the income-tax liability of the members. Although throughout history we have seen the Christian faith up to combating such successfully, today we do not seem willing to challenge that, or is our faith too weak?

That lead me to examine "The Gospel according To Obama", and attached are my thoughts on that. Considering this as background and then relating it to the functioning of our over-sized government that Obama is devoted to, we can see it incorporated the rank materialism of socialist governments, subordinating those rights and freedoms we all cherish and which were covenanted to us by our founders in the Constitution.

President Obama is a convenient Christian. He believes in the Bible when it is convenient and political. He firmly believes that we should render unto Caesar what is Caesar's but over looks that we should render unto God what is God's and to God's people. He believes and orders we should render everything unto Caesar and then let the socialist Caesar decide on not only the pittance to go to the people but also who should receive that pittance. (Reference: Matthew Chapter 22-21.)

Matthew speaks to that which is the people (Chap. 20-15) "Is it not lawful for me to do what I will with my own? Is thine eye evil because I am good?" President Reagan, who had been a Sunday school teacher, may have used this sense of evil when he referred to the Soviet's as being an evil empire.

Before becoming a disciple, Matthew was a tax collector, and he knew very well he could not collect taxes where there was no wherewithal. Caesar can take only where the consumption is less than the production, which production corning first. "Give us this day our daily bread!"

In the Old Testament, the book of Deuteronomy can be considered the gospel of entitlements, where our Lord promises us all kinds of benefits if we are good but much harm if we are bad. It has been called the Book of Blessings and Curses! But we must look to Matthew for how we can earn our entitlements, preaching with parables and principles that man has a duty to be diligent and to use all his talents, skills and energy in producing that which is good and needed. Those who are deficient in this are termed "the least of these" (which, too often is interpreted as meaning "the poor--- a gross error made by 4,000 ministers who ran a full-page advertisement in a Washington newspaper in July 2011!).

We should be very suspicious of a person who claims he had regularly worshipped under the guidance of Reverend Wright, who was not only located on the south side of Chicago but who also was on the south side of conventional Christian teaching

This is a Judeo-Christian country. The Supreme Court has said at least three times that this is a Christian nation. It has prospered when it has cleaved to Christian principles. But Socialism is not Christianity; it is secular sovereignty. For this nation to receive the blessing set forth in Deuteronomy we must follow the message of Matthew if we are to earn those blessings. Our leadership must be dedicated to this in both thoughts and actions.

CHAPTER TWENTY-TWO

GAAP AND GOVERNMENT ACCOUNTING PRINCIPLES: THEY VIOLATE DUE PROCESS AND ARE UNCONSTITUTIONAL.

The development of generally-accepted accounting principle over five centuries. Coincidental with the discovery of America in 1492, double-entry bookkeeping was discovered by Italians. Double-entry bookkeeping gave rise to the art of disciplined accounting in the Western World, establishing a solid system for the recording of ownership of property and the income.

This was a basic and necessary tool for America under its new government where all ownership of property and the income therefrom belonged to the people, with the people having both the right and also the responsibility to account for it, and the government would have only limited property and income to the extent needed by a limited government, but even here in governing there were absolutely no reasons why an honest and open government would need any other accounting principles.

In 1913 the taxation of income put a new emphasis on the correct calculation of income. But nobody at that time had even the remotest idea of what would happen here or that the government would inject itself into this private area.

Fortunately, by 1913 this country had considerable expertise in the art and practice of accounting, and an excellent profession to oversee and discipline it had been started. Certified public accountants (CPAs) were being registered by the states and the practice of independent public accounting was well underway, much of this based on the Chartered Accountants of England. The practitioners in-the art in 1913 naturally felt that they would have an important part to play in the administration of this new federal law. But they were sorely mistaken, and were swept under by the bad federal legislation that followed.

The professional public accounting associations and their principles had been accepted with little question. Undoubtedly, they expected Generally Accepted Accounting Principles (GAAP) would have a very direct part to play in the upcoming process. But the result was chaos and calamity.

In Washington, the "statesmen" in their zeal to maximize tax revenues shoved GAAP aside and invented their own accounting rules. And at the same time, some of these "statesmen" could not resist the forces of special interest, and so they passed rules and laws permitting reductions and deferring of taxes otherwise due. This, of course, presented a quandary to the CPAs who were obligated to certify the correctness of the financial statements. As a result we now have balance sheets sprinkled with new assets and new liabilities—prepaid taxes and deferred taxes—and this makes the financial statements more difficult to understand, particularly where there are also and frequently long notes disclosing that questions have been raised about income taxes often going back several years. The actual, realistic tax liability is up in the air in too many cases.

But big Government was not through; this was not enough. In 2002, Congress passed the Sarbanes-Oxley Act. To put this in the proper perspective, however, two things must be noted. First, financial statements are the joint product of two professions, accounting and legal, with both being responsible for the contents. Secondly, going back to the 1970s with the Chrysler financial failure, Congress had fallen into the trap of believing that when large corporations failed, irrespective of the causes, the federal government must intervene as a matter of national interest. And as part of this, Congress also attributes to itself the knowledge and skills required to fix it!

The basic problem is that the Congress and the Bush administration failed to promote free and open competition among industries. They instead permitted many corporations to become so large that they had become monopolies, and they in turn because of their size had been unable to survive in what remained of a competitive economy. Although started over 100 years before this, Congress had noted these distinct possibilities and had passed antitrust and other laws to limit and hold this down, with sporadic prosecution during that century to limit and break up the more egregious examples of it.

Also undoubtedly one factor pushing the Congress to pass this sweeping Sarbanes-Oxley Act was that it still had a bad taste in its mouth from the Enron case, and some of them still sensed that the resolution of that case had been highly unsatisfactory and injudicious. This included that the public outcry from Enron had caused the destruction of a credible accounting firm, Arthur Andersen, with over 13,000 auditors losing their jobs. Unfortunately, it was only later, when it hit the Supreme Court, that the injustice was publicly noted.

The financial statements of most all businesses require authentication because there is a widespread use of that information with many "third parties" having a legitimate interest. The consumers of financial statements rely on this joint product of the auditor and lawyers; there is a "silent contract" between these professionals to produce a dependable product. The lawyer's tangible part of this is presented to the auditors in their representation letter which the auditor insists on receiving before giving an opinion. But there is a serious flaw here.

That letter usually comes from legal counsel for the business. This was noted in the foregoing, commenting on the Enron case. All this legitimately raises this question: Should there not also be a profession and practice of "independent public lawyers" to give their opinion alongside that of the "independent public accountant?

Congress, in passing the Sarbanes-Oxley Act, picked on the most visible target – certified public accountants. But lawmakers overlooked the actual cause: the absence of fair and free competition. If that had been taken care of, we would no longer have these "too big to fail" bombs. The Sarbanes-Oxley Act made a mountain out of a molehill. True, there are some punishable accounting and auditing practices, but this was a case of needless overkill. Lawmakers prescribed a mountain of sanctions, including prosecution of corporate board members.

The following is extracted from my critical report, "The Sarbanes-Oxley Mistake," written in January 2011, almost a decade after passage of the Act. It was possible by then to see the effects the law had on financial reporting and statements. I sent a copy to my alma mater, the College of Business at the University of Illinois; my comments were in response to an article in the College's "Perspectives" publication.

Here it is first timely to note that for many years this College of Business had a top rating in the area of accountancy, but these "Perspectives" made it clear that it too had succumbed to Big Government and was no longer interested in producing true professionals in accounting principles and practices or auditors to assure adherence to that.

The basic question: Why should our government that cannot provide its citizens with accurate and honest accounting and reporting on its fiscal affairs inject itself upon the private sector and tell it how it should do its accounting and financial reporting? The Sarbanes-Oxley Act was supposed to be a giant step forward in the reform of corporate accounting reporting; instead, it has been a giant step backward, costly and unproductive.

The great importance of proper accounting and financial reporting.

Ever since graduating with accountancy major from the University of Illinois in 1934, I have been a producer and consumer of the products of accounting and financial reporting. This has given me time to reflect on the true nature of accountancy today.

Accountants are the handmaiden of the law. The invention of double-entry bookkeeping (1492) cemented that relationship, citing that existing between assets, claims against the assets, and the owner's equity in those assets. Financial statements are essentially legal in nature but also involve an understanding of economics and the actions of the market. Although historical, their value is in being forward looking. The practitioners in the art are also professionals with defined standards of expertise, discipline and ethics.

Through the years, beginning in Europe, accountants and lawyers had been working together to supply the demand for financial statements by "third parties" that they could trust, and this produced a "silent contract" between them that they would work together as fiduciaries in the process. Thus, the financial statements of a business are the joint products of accountants and lawyers, both within the corporation and then later in the auditing and certifying process. Auditors will not deliver an opinion until they receive a rather broad and comprehensive representation letter from the lawyers with respect to the legal proprieties of the statements. These representation letters in almost all cases are those from the legal counsel for the corporation. This has been accepted without exception on the basis that all such legal counsel when admitted to the bar become, in effect, "officers of the court" and their integrity cannot be questioned. But in the highly complex, multi-millions, billions, trillions atmosphere today, this may very well be subjected to question. Should not the auditors also receive a confirming opinion and legal representations from "independent public lawyers".

The assuring "opinions" now appearing in most financial statements typically cover several pages, come from the auditors and are confirmed by top corporate officials. This is becoming rather standardized "boiler plate." But in all of this, the "third parties" such as investors are looking for just one assurance which is that "the financial statements present fairly in all material respects the results of operations and the financial condition. This used to be (with only minor exceptions) that the basic standard was "generally-accepted accounting principles" (GAAP), but we are now in a never-never land of confusion, of committees and oversight boards, plus the courts being involved because of all of this chaos. As honest financial statements are the lubricants upon which businesses operate, we now have debilitating friction of all kinds.

Issuers of financial statements are now in a quandary, and knock themselves out trying to produce something functional but not incriminating, operating under, strong legal constraints.

With financial statements today running close to 100 pages and with the "opinions" letters covering three to four pages, typically, we can clearly see the unintended consequences of Sarbanes-Oxley, and all of its regulatory trappings. That was the gist of my critical letter sent to the University of Illinois. I received no answer. Perhaps it was not understood, or perhaps they have no legitimate answer!

Returning to the "Perspectives" article, the accounting professors presented a very weak case in support of the Act and its effects. The Supreme Court case they cited raised rather narrow issues and there was actually a split decision. An alumnus of the College of Business was a principal in bringing this case. He stated "the Act is one of the worst laws we have seen in a long time. It has caused an enormous amount of accounting work for businesses.' I've talked to a lot of CEOs who say it causes them tremendous stress. Even honest mistakes can lead to criminal penalties."

Most upsetting about the article was when it started to question the diligence, honesty and integrity of both auditors and businessmen. Their inference was clearly the most businessmen are bad, and that they covered up the "badness" by the way they had the transactions recorded in the accounts! Accordingly, if the auditors were truly diligent they would uncover all of this "badness" if they worked long and hard enough. They even proposed a "bonus" for finding errors whenever they found such errors over and above what they were already receiving for doing the job right! In effect, the professors condemned businessmen as a class!

But the article did not follow through to the logical conclusion from these allegations. If all CEOs and businessmen are "bad" the solution proposed of tighter and more internal control would still leave these bad actors working together! Of course, they would still issue the same kind of "opinion" letters assuring everybody that everything was fine.

In my over 50 years of experience in business I found with very few exceptions that almost all successful businessmen have integrity. Without it, their businesses could not have succeeded. (As an aside, I must note that many of these alleged dishonest people were graduates and the products of the College of Business of the University of Illinois!)

Citing the constitutionality of the Act, the head of the accountancy department apparently believes that the Act has been a very positive step forward. According to him, the recent global financial crisis exposed weaknesses in corporate financial accounting and reporting, despite Sarbanes-Oxley. As correct readings of the facts are partially set forth in the following, this "crisis" was caused by much, much more than accounting, good or bad.

The "Perspectives" article alleged that prior to this Act, accountants were guided primarily by standards established by industry associations, and "the auditing profession had been largely self-regulated," The article continued that self regulation proved costly in the wake of corporate scandals--World Com, Enron, Tyco International, and Adelphia Communications. With the economy in a downturn and the stock market experiencing dizzying gyrations, the public and politicians demanded stricter financial oversight of U.S. companies. Sarbanes-Oxley was the result. Remember, this was 2002, prior to the housing price collapse that started in 2007.

The Article explained the main parts of the law as follows:

Under the law, much more detailed disclosures are required of companies. Senior executives also have to take individual responsibility for accuracy of financial reports. The Public Company Accounting Oversight Board (PCAOB), which was created as part of Sarbanes-Oxley, established detailed processes for audits as well as procedures for inspection and enforcement. Sarbanes-Oxley increased penalties for fraud and it made the failure to certify corporate financial reports a criminal offense.

The article alleged with little support that there have been too many auditing failures and declines in quality of auditing. It did mention a few cases, including Enron but as set forth herein that was caused by failures much broader than accounting and auditing. The accountants failing to obey all of the rules were minor parts, a view affirmed by the Supreme Court's finding on Enron.

The Act wields a big stick over accountants and anybody having anything to do with accounting, but fear never accomplishes very much and results in unintended consequences. The unintended consequences have included producing principally financial statements containing several thousand words of "opinion" reassurances and mountains and masses of financial detail, leaving the customers of financial statement much worse off than ever. The financial "house" is covered over and plastered with so much roofing and siding and shrubbery that we cannot see the house. Materiality, which is what we look for, is hidden in the mass of figures.

Further, the government here again is guilty of its own fatal conceit always resulting in deceit. The Oversight Board and Committees established to do this plastering job are mostly political appointments, many with professional expertise to be questioned.

Further, there already were well-established and accepted government agencies, such as the Securities and Exchange Commission over 50 years in existence, which had long exercised oversight in this area, without threatening fear and punishment to the producers of financial statements. Such regulatory overlap only confuses business and the security markets generally. The SEC should have maintained its direct oversight.

As stated, this "Perspectives" article was completely wrong when it criticized that until this Act was passed "accountants were guided by standards established by industry association. Until the law was passed, the auditing profession had been largely self-regulated." Throughout the past century the auditing profession had developed effective associations that promulgated standards and principles that were adjusted constantly to the changing nature of business and the economy.

A good example of this was the McKesson and Robbins case in the 1930's when the auditors participation in the inventory-taking process was enlarged. We have long had the American Institute of Public Accountants and the Financial Accounting Standards Board. And academia had its American Accounting Association.

Self-regulation in a profession is not a negative, especially as it has been done in auditing and accounting. It is quite responsive to needs and changing conditions, and where the associations are relatively independent the results are much better than when the heavy-handed government attempts to do the job, where politics and self-interests are always in play. I repeat, the self-regulation here has been a positive, not a negative, in the great advances that have been made in auditing, accounting and financial reporting.

It cannot be denied that for many years AICPA and FASB did very effective work and their generally-accepted accounting principles were exactly that and understandable. States have accountancy boards and they are principally engaged in licensing the practice of public accountants and do nothing in the area of accounting and auditing principles and standards. They also help in administering of CPA examinations but have no part in writing them. These examinations include a section on business Law to make sure those licensed have a comprehensive understanding of it.

Here it can be noted that not surprisingly the GAAP purists, hoping that the true accounting religion would survive, have been further mistreated by Big Government's uncivilized decimation of sound accounting. This was caused by such perversions as "fair-value accounting." They established this as an integral part of GAAP several years before the current financial crisis started. That this is a grievous mistake has been amply supported by ex-banker John A. Allison in his late 2012 book "The Financial Crisis and the Free-Market Cure." In a chapter "Fair-Value Accounting and Wealth Destruction," it starts out saying it all. "There are a multitude of problems with fair-value accounting. Conceptually, the major issue is that adjusting a business's income statement based on random fluctuations in its balance sheet of its assets and liabilities distorts operating earning and provides misleading and confusing information about the underlying earnings power." In the next fourteen pages, there is solid support to show how it helps destroy wealth, employing a comprehensive knowledge of economics, accounting, banking, and almost everything else related to the proper management of finance in a free-market country. Allison concludes: "It would be very interesting if the United States had a private accounting system, as it did in the century before 1935. The systems(s) would be based on theory detached from reality...

The biggest advantage is that the private accounting system would be non-political."

Allison's great and timely book also supports my criticism of the Sarbanes-Oxley Act. In chapter 13, "The Myth that Deregulation Caused the Financial Crisis", he states:

"The financial industry was not deregulated, it was misregulated: During the Bush administration, three major new financial regulatory acts were passed: The Privacy Act, Sarbanes-Oxley, and the Patriot Act. The primary regulatory focus was initially on Sarbanes-Oxley and then on the Patriot Act. Sarbanes-Oxley is the legislation passed by Congress as a result of the Enron and WorldCom scandals to theoretically eliminate accounting fraud. The financial industry has been operating under its own "Sarbanes-Oxley" since the thrift crisis of the early 1990s. Sarbanes-Oxley is a redundant system on top of a redundant system. In the case of BB&T, our internal auditors are audited by our external auditors, the NC State Banking Examiners, the Federal Deposit Insurance Corporation (FDIC), and the Federal Reserve. These are auditors auditing auditors auditing auditors. There is not a shred of evidence that Sarbanes-Oxley reduced fraud by one penny during the financial crisis. However, it did significantly misdirect management's attention from the real risk in the financial industry."

The assuring "opinions" now appearing in most financial statements typically cover several pages, come from the auditors must be confirmed by top corporate officials. This is becoming rather standardized "boiler plate." But in all of this, the "third parties" such as investors are looking for just one assurance which is that "the financial statements present fairly in all material respects the results of operations and the financial condition. This used to be (with only minor exceptions) that the basic standard was "generally-accepted accounting principles (GAAP), but we are now in a never-never land of confusion, or committees and oversight boards, plus the courts being involved because of all of this chaos. As honest financial statements are the lubricants upon which businesses operate, we now have debilitating friction of all kinds.

Issuers of financial statements are now in a quandary, and knock themselves out trying to produce something functional but not incriminating, operating under strong legal constraints.

With financial statements today running close to 100 pages and with the "opinions" letters covering three to four pages, typically, we can clearly see the unintended consequences of Sarbanes-Oxley, and all of its regulatory trappings. That was the gist of my critical letter sent to the University of Illinois. I received no answer. Perhaps it was not understood, or perhaps they have no legitimate answer!

Returning to the "Perspectives" article, the accounting professors presented a very weak case in support of the Act and its effects. The Supreme Court case they cited raised rather narrow issues and there was actually a split decision. An alumnus of the College of Business was a principal in bringing this case. He stated "the Act is one of the worst laws we have seen in a long time. It has caused an enormous amount of accounting work for businesses. I've talked to a lot of CEOs who say it causes them tremendous stress. Even honest mistakes can lead to criminal penalties."

Most upsetting about the article was when it started to question the diligence, honesty and integrity of both auditors and businessmen. Their inference was clearly the most businessmen are bad, and that they covered up the "badness" by the way they had the transactions recorded in the accounts! Accordingly, if the auditors were truly diligent they would uncover all of this "badness" if they worked long and hard enough. They even proposed a "bonus" for finding errors whenever they found such errors over and above what they were already receiving for doing the job right! In effect, the professors condemned businessmen as a class!

Comparing corporate annual reports and financial statements before and after Sarbanes-Oxley results in a serious indictment of the Act. Before we had fairly concise documents where materiality of information was stressed and details were subordinated.

Here are three examples of the kinds of financial reports the Act has been producing. These are two moderate-sized corporations and one very large one. The first example comes from my old company Kennametal Inc., for the year ended June 30, 2012, which consisted of the Form 10-K filed with the Securities and Exchange Commission, plus eight pages of supplemental financial data. Included were two "opinion" reports, "Report of Independent Accounting Firm", a full page signed by Price Waterhouse Cooper LLP, and Management's Report on Internal Control Over Financial Reporting" (not signed), which stated the auditors had audited the effectiveness of internal control. These were followed by 47 pages of very detailed financial statements. The balance sheet contained prepaid income taxes (assets) and deferred income taxes (liabilities.), with a note on income taxes covering three pages.

The second example is The J. M. Smucker Company's report for the year ended April 30, 2012, which contained 60 pages which in large part duplicated its Form 10-K. It contained two "opinion" pages signed by the auditors, "Report of Independent Registered Public Accounting Firm on Internal Control", and "Report of Independent Registered Public Accounting Firm on the Consolidated Financial Statements." On a separate page, the two top corporate officials signed a "Report of Management on Internal Control over Financial Reporting", followed by another page where the two top corporate officials had signed a "Report of Management on Responsibility for Financial Reporting." There were four pages of "opinion" letters.

The third comes from Exxon Mobil for 2011, which published a roughly 75-page "plain paper" called "Financial Statements and Supplemental Information." Being so huge, it evidently felt comfortable minimizing the "opinion" reporting, reducing that to two pages--a very brief "Management's Report on Internal Control Over Financial Reporting", signed by three officials, and a "Report of Independent Public Accounting Firm on Internal Control", and "Report of Independent Registered Public Accounting Firm." It started out assuring that the financial statement were "in conformity with accounting principles accepted in the United States of America", and further that "the Corporation maintained in all material respects effective internal control over financial reporting as of December 31, 2011, based on criteria established in the Treadway Commission's broadside on internal control". An explanatory paragraph then explained what internal control over financial reporting really is, and then concluded with that qualification which casts serious doubt on everything.

Is the Sarbanes-Oxley Act unconstitutional? As previously noted, accountants in late-15th century Italy devised double-entry bookkeeping to reflect the ownership of property in their accounts. Since then, there has been an implicit, unwritten contract between accountants and lawyers: Accountants would be the loyal handmaidens of the lawyers, and each would be dedicated to reflect correctly the ownership of that property.

Under our Constitution, that contract is continued, underwritten and guaranteed. The accounting profession has through the years developed generally-accepted accounting principles and similar disciplines, all in conformance with and approval of the legal profession. But then our Congress has rewritten and negated those disciplines, establishing new rules for accountants that, despite good intentions, effectively cancel the classical contract between accountants and lawyers.

The Congress can pass laws only insofar as they are constitutional. But in passing the Sarbanes-Oxley Law, lawmakers created an unconstitutional law. To the extent that law forces accountants and lawyers to do things that their professional disciplines do not countenance, that violates their constitutional right to establish a contract, not to mention violation of the due process requirements surrounding the contract.

There is a very strong case that the Sarbanes-Oxley Law is in violation of our Constitution. But the adverse approach and practices that it mandates are such that, on its own, it is a bad law. It is helping to support the overreach of the federal government into the private sector.

Is the auditor's opinion an anomaly? As previously noted herein, when we attempt to record our wealth we use the art of accountancy to record the stream of transactions involved in our receiving the goods and services we desire. Then when people personally or in their businesses wish to obtain assurances as to the correctness of this recording, auditors are retained to give their professional opinions.

Today when it is the intention of the auditor to give a "clean" (unqualified) opinion, that opinion appears to have become an anomaly. That has been caused by the efforts of government to increase the personal liability of the auditor (but it seems not that of the legal counsel, overlooking the fact that the accountant is the handmaiden of the law!)

The usual opinion consists of a statement by the auditor of work done and the conclusions (sometimes in reverse, the PriceWaterhouse Coopers model). But in this the auditor may have overreached because of the terminology used. Instead of stating the financial statements fairly present historically the results of operations for the period and the balance sheet as of the end of the period, they use the term "financial condition". This contains the representation that financially the business entity is so adequately strong that it will have a continuing profitable existence. But the auditor is not a fortune teller or a psychic. But now the auditor has a second thought, recognizing that he must give major weight to the system of internal control exercised by the business, the importance of which was intensified by the recent governmental regulations and laws. And so the auditor in almost all cases now adds the qualification (which contains a sub-rosa insult of management):

"Because of its inherent limitations, internal control over financial reporting may not prevent or detect misstatements. Also, projections of any evaluation of effectiveness as to future periods are subject to the risk that controls may become inadequate because of changes in conditions, or that the degree of compliance with policies and procedures may deteriorate."

The auditor's continuing but terminal responsibility date is that of the date of the opinion, usually a very short period after the balance sheet date. For this period the professional work of the auditor consists merely of a review, not an audit.

Thus in using "financial condition" the auditor is really making a representation about the future and ongoing good health of the business. But then, recognizing the impossibility of any such representation, the auditor adds the final qualification noted above.

But in the interest of intellectual integrity, I must add the following to my stated conclusion. The future of all business operations (both profit and nonprofit) depends on an infinite number of variables, and there has been no demand that the auditor note them in his opinion or even refer to them broadly. So why should he be required to note only one of such variables (internal control)?

Further the art of the professional auditor, like that of the professional painter, is to use his skills in setting forth in a concise picture that which is material in understanding the financial condition and results of operations.

Investors know they are on their own in making investments but in performing this task like all others they need practical tools. The financial statements today do not fulfill practical need, thanks to Sarbanes-Oxley among other things.

Here is a final, common sense solution to this quandary. I repeat my supported conclusion: "Sarbanes-Oxley should be repealed and the profession of accounting should be given back its professional status." Let the private sector have its tools so that it can perform its functions properly, efficiently, something that the government cannot do (or force us to do).

And this final step is for the auditor and his client to disclose in their reports that they have entered into a continuing agreement under which the review of internal control would be ongoing, continuing into the following year. Then should this agreement be terminated; the client would have a duty to inform its owners and the public that had taken place.

Has the legal profession discharged its full duty to the people? The foregoing presents a strong case that the lawyers both in their professional practice and in their dominance in the legislative process have sorely mistreated the accountants. The accountants should now be crying loudly "Rape!!" and demanding to live outside the big, bad government's house of prostitution.

Conclusion. The evidence is clear. The federal government, in carrying out the income tax amendment, has corrupted proper accounting and redefined income so broadly that it is almost meaningless. And then in its attempts to control the private sector and prevent business cycles, financial crises and depressions, it has corrupted proper, accepted accounting, making financial statements of little use. In so doing, it has violated the Constitution.

But the commonsense, constitutional solution to this problem would be that which I gave for the Sarbanes-Oxley Act: repeal. This mountain of controls and paperwork should be eliminated, and the accounting profession should be given back its contractual freedom: Let the private sector have its tools so that it can perform its functions properly and efficiently, something the government cannot force it to do.

The evidence is clear. The federal government, in creating and carrying out the income tax amendment, has corrupted proper accounting by redefining "income" so broadly as to be almost meaningless. And then in its attempts to use all of this to prevent business cycles, financial crises and depressions, it has only corrupted accounting and has made financial statements of little use. And in all of these failures this big, bad government has failed and has violated our Constitution.

A DECLARATION OF INDEPENDENCE

BY THE INDEPENDENT PUBLIC ACCOUNTLNTS

To the American people:

In the course of human events when it becomes necessary to complain, it is our duty to explain the reasons.

Although for a very long time we have been independent public accountants, dictators in Washington now have forced us to give up our God-given rights to be independent public accountants. We must issue opinions exactly as they mandate.

These dictators expect us to continue our traditional practice, set forth in a page of righteous rhetoric, that we have examined the books and records of our client, and that in making that audit we have crossed all of the t's and dotted all of i's, but now upon order of these holy saints in Washington (some of whom have not even recently treaded their way to church) we cannot certify but must do much more, supplying many financial details, and obtain signed certifications from top officers of the client. But even after that, we are required to question if our client and its management can be wholly trusted in its presentation of financial condition inasmuch as the apparent solid financial condition they represent deteriorate in the future because of failure by the client to keep them active. This possibility then must be set forth in a final paragraph.

The final package we are asked to sign is to certify to this voluminous amount of financial information and not only the results of operation and financial condition. This is not an "opinion"; this is an obfuscation, and has the value of that!

We ask all patriots to join us in restoring our independent rights of being independent public accountants, helping us in our pursuit of Life, Liberty and Happiness.

CHAPTER TWENTY-THREE

THE COMPLETE SUPREME COURT

The most important part of our government is the judiciary. On this, the Constitution is brief. Article III, Section 1, says: "The Judicial Power of the united States shall be vested in the Supreme Court and in such Courts as the congress may from time to time ordain and establish." Section 2 merely clarifies the jurisdiction of the Court. The entire Article III covers only a bit more than one page, far less than the sections covering the legislative and executive branches.

It must be recognized that the Founders when addressing the judiciary were facing entirely new and unique situations. They were used to and had accepted the judicial process as carried out in the colony-states, reflecting the English background where the courts were directly under the ruler, and that was the judiciary. But here the rulers were the people. That may account for the fact that Article III was devoted almost exclusively to the courts and the Supreme Court. It gave it power over all whereas in actual practice it properly has been only an appellate court, the top one.

The Founders were certainly aware of the guiding principles and purposes in writing the Constitution and perhaps assumed the new judiciary and its courts would be aware of all of that, and that basic philosophy would be all that was needed in carrying out the judiciary function, assuring justice for all of the people.

The following may be repetitious but perhaps be needed for clarification and to make us remember the historical origins and antecedents of which lead to the Constitution and are imbedded in it. The original preamble to that document was in the writings of the 17th and 18th century of those who gave us the Enlightenment, pulling us out of the Middle Ages. That was the basis of and the preamble to the Declaration of Independence, and this consisted of many complaints against the English king, and set forth the basic propositions that the people in governing themselves were all equal, and in all other areas of their lives they were equal in having the freedom of the inalienable rights given us by our Creator. And that declaration after giving us independence became the preamble to the Constitution. But in writing the actual preamble they did not state the prime objective of establishing a unique new country, and they started out with what the pursuits would be after that nation was established. They most likely considered this not necessary because the vivid details were still fresh in their minds.

It does appear perhaps the reason Article III did not expand on the functions of the judiciary was that the Founders assumed that the learned members of the bar presiding over the courts would be well aware of these historical antecedents and would use that as their guiding principles in administering justice, , a judiciary of solid principles and not those of ruler-appointed and controlled courts.

Viewed in the totality of the Constitution, the judiciary is not a single and disparate function of government but all three parts. It has the vital reviewing power. It is really the indispensable glue that holds it all together, assuring that all parts are operating smoothly and in unison as they should, for a single purpose. That means the Supreme Court itself must be in unison--there can be no split decisions. For our laws to be valid they must be stated so they are clear to all our citizens; they are not optional. When the Supreme Court renders split decisions, it is not at all supreme. It should return the law to its source for clarification. If it then be returned with no substantive change, the nine justices are faced with "controversies", and Article III contemplated that. That does not means we are returning to a government of people and not of principles because there are rock-solid principles, our inalienable rights, and there are the standards to guide them. They should not stretch and improvise as they frequently do. But too frequently when there does not appear any law or established equity to cover, they think they are in a wilderness.

But here we should heed carefully the warnings of Aristotle previously cited herei--that intellectuals when given powers are tempted and frequently do forget and subordinate justice to that resulting in what he called the "worst" of actions by this political animal.

From the Austrian School, Friedrich A. Hayek in a lengthy essay in 1949, "The Intellectuals and Socialism" covered those same human failures comprehensively, bringing it up to date. This essay begins:

"In all democratic countries, in the United States even more than elsewhere, a strong belief prevails that the influence of the intellectuals on politics is negligible. This is no doubt true of the power of intellectuals to make their peculiar opinions of the moment influence decisions, of the extent to which they can sway the popular vote on questions on which they differ from the current views of the masses. Yet over somewhat longer periods they have probably never exercised so great an influence as they do today in those countries. This power they wield by shaping public opinion."

He then differentiates these pretend-intellectuals from the legitimate, calling the former "secondhand dealers in ideas."'

Hayek makes no reference to Aristotle or to the Constitution; there was no need for this as they are part of his own "pedigree." He does refer to several respected economists, not for their ideas but in support of his. He notes that intellectuals are in fact a "fairly new phenomenon of history", and that with the widespread education of the populace creates an environment where ideas are accepted without too much examination of their soundness or quality. Further, it is not enough for "the man of affairs" to know from practical experience that socialism cannot work concluding "So long as the intellectual gets the better of the argument, the most valid objections of the specific issue will be brushed aside."

He paraphrases and adds to Aristotle when he says: "It may be that a free society as we have known it carries in itself the forces of its own destruction, that freedom achieved is taken for granted and ceases to be valued, and that the free growth of ideas which is the essence of a free society will bring about the destruction of the foundation on which it depend." Hayek concludes: "We must make the building of a free society once more an intellectual adventure, a deed of courage."

Larry P. Arnn, president of Hillsdale College, deserves a good measure of credit for the ideas I have been expressing. Much of this comes from his recent book: "The Founders' Key: The Divine and Natural Connection between the Declaration and the Constitution." He reminds us that the revolt against King George III "was about more than economics." The Colonies took up arms to assume "separate and equal station to which the Laws of Nature and Nature's God entitled them." The Continental Congress "conveyed the essential attributes of the government necessary to secure those rights."

Arnn is arguing that the Founders had an idealistic faith in the people to defend their liberties. But the effective checks and balances against the concentration of executive branch power are dissipating. President Obama appears more interested in consolidating power than enforcing the law in an even-handed way. The department is quite mute when the public calls on it for many important matters. In the face of this, the Supreme Court should take over certain government functions. It is within this context where I favor the Supreme Court to be an active court, not in shaping our laws but in their enforcement. Although the individual justices have little power, collectively they have great power, in fact, responsibility, to step in when the laws of the land are not being carried out.

To repeat, the Constitution neatly divides the sovereign power of government into three parts, and in the operations it is also divided into three parts. All these parts are expected to cooperate and work smoothly together. But constantly and daily we see gross failures here. That is why the Supreme Court must be the indispensable glue working to hold all of it together, insisting on cooperation and coordinated operation. But in its actual operations today it does little but the mechanical matching and comparison of laws with the Constitution (far removed from the Bill of Rights or of all of the other rights of man that are in it, written and unwritten).

Today we have an unworkable system, with no mechanics to fix it. It is a system that has stolen from the people the very tools they thought they had to repair it. It also has permitted the mechanics to loaf on the job and not use those tools.

To Summarize. It is the job of the Supreme Court to discharge the complete judicial function, which is "to judge." And in judging it is "The Judge", but in judging it has a precise book of standards, standards which determine precisely what kinds of laws are ordered by a free people in governing themselves. But man being imperfect, there will always be imperfections. And the people must be protected from their imperfections, and this is what the Constitution tries to do but upon review we see it provides no discipline to see that is actually done. The Founders worried about that, wondering whether that document was too weak, but Madison consoled them by optimistically expecting the cool deliberations of the community, expecting forced corrections. They did not realize what a strong and complete document they had written. In that document setting forth very little language on the judiciary, they left the perfect remedy where it should be, in the Court. As I have reasoned herein, the Supreme Court must be considered the disciplinarian, the enforcer, always the job of the courts. Thus, perhaps by default, the Supreme Court is supreme not only in judging the laws, but more importantly what they must be if the Constitution is to have sustenance and continuity. The Supreme Court is the "The Judge", and it has the ultimate power in defining definitely what the law can be, which all branches of government, the states and the people must obey.

The essential nature of laws and what they really do must be recognized. Laws are both the enemies and protectors of free men, and consequently we must look here first before judging whether any specific proposed law is a proper part of this government if man be permitted the unfettered pursuit of his freedom. The laws passed must be consonant in balance with this to promote his morality that is an essential part of our Constitution. But this establishes only a very broad-base standard, and here is where the Supreme Court has a constitutional obligation in that in reviewing any enacted law the first thing it must do is to determine whether on its face it meets this ultimate standard of promoting freedom. But when the Court looks only at specifics in a mechanical matching process, this is not its complete job. Thus, its job is really to complete the Constitution by enunciating the unquestioned Rights that must be followed, written and unwritten. Based on this reasoning, the Bill of Rights amendments must be considered as merely examples of the established whole. Laws do not and cannot create new rights; they can only affirm the existing rights or impose penalties and mandate corrections where rights have been violated. But most of the laws being passed today, extending the long arms of government, are entirely different; they take away some of the established rights or create new rights, supported usually by combinations of emotions, special interest, and thrust for partisan power. The Supreme Court must be adamant in attacking this slaughter of our natural human rights.

PART 5

RESTORATION OF OUR CONSTITUTIONAL RIGHTS. PRIVATIZATION OF RETIREMENT INCOME AND HEALTH CARE

Introduction To Part Five

In the United States of America, the people have been given personal rights, but during the past 100 years they have been removed, especially in the area of retirement and health care. The creation and expansion of Social Security to enormous entitlement programs might not have been contemplated by the people who created them, but it is up to us to right this situation.

Our federal government in 1935 initiated a system of taxation mandating forced savings by all, the uses of which were to alleviate the hardships among many caused by old age, health care, and unemployment. This was prompted by the extreme hardships inflicted by the Great Depression. It was enacted as a modest social insurance program, but since then it has grown monstrously and has become a mechanism for massive income redistribution. We have been led to believe that individuals must look to the government for salvation. Accordingly, it is now considered an "entitlement" program.

The twin entitlements of Social Security and Medicare are extracting large portions of our GDP. Not only has there been out-sized benefit promises but under-sized provisions for funding them. And the funds that have been contributed have been dishonestly handled and spent on expanding the size of government operations and not invested in trust funds.

The basic economic principles behind Social Security and Medicare were sound but the implementation was not. When people foresee a future personal need they save and invest to cover it. That, of course, requires a surplus of their current production over their current consumption, to provide the funds for investment.

But government took over these functions for its people because it felt people were not smart or provident enough to take care of themselves. History has shown how false and baseless that is, showing that when people assume power they frequently forget about principles. It certainly has not worked in the United States or any other country.

The only true "entitlement" is one that is earned by the recipient and has accepted the obligation to fund it. But the government has no resources and can do no funding. It must look to the taxpayers to pay current benefits and to hold and invest the funds to cover this growing liability while it accrues. Therein we have the potential for collapse.

In early 2005, in support of the valiant efforts of President Bush to reform Social Security, I sent him a 30-page manuscript: "Social Security Reform--Its Time Is now." The White House acknowledged receipt. In September 2011, renewing my efforts, I wrote a lengthy paper: "At Last! A Retirement Income Plan That Provides Social and Private Security." In 2012 with the presidential campaign, entitlements hit the front page. This prompted me to prepare a way to privatize Social Security and Medicare, which also would be applicable to the new Obamacare law now being implemented.

Here is an outline of my plan, which assumes that intelligent people anticipate their future needs and save for them.

The funding for these future needs will be deposited by the participants, whether employed or unemployed, into savings accounts in reasonable and restricted amounts. To the extent they come from sources that are subject to income taxes they will be funded from that taxable income. Most of this now comes out of the workers compensation and is sent directly to the government. This will be discontinued and the amount authorized by the employee will go directly to him (or as he directs). The employer's match will be phased out over a short period. Funds in these savings accounts will be invested and the yield will accrue and compound exempt from income taxes, all of this being owned and controlled by the participant.

The disbursements from these tax-advantaged accounts will be restricted to their stated objectives. They will be determined by the owners in a free-market mode, making choices in their best interests and using providers competitively operating in that free-market mode. Thus the traditional relation of man with his professional will be restored among other very beneficial things. This will include the use of private insurance (as he has used it for centuries) to shift risks he cannot afford to insurers with adequate resources, all at competitive premiums, actuarially defined. And the lengths of these contracts will correspond to lengths of the existence of these observed unaffordable risks.

The only part of government in this will be to enact and enforce laws that will implement and encourage all of this. That includes the responsibility of making more certain a healthy economy in which people can safely invest, and that will include at all times and in all industries healthy competition.

What will be the result of these radical changes on the entire economy? It will be huge, but few people now see it. These entitlements alone have diverted productive resources to unproductive government uses to the extent of more than 20 percent, and when related other entitlements and regulatory controls are factored in, this will well exceed 25 percent.

In becoming a welfare state, this nation has incurred a huge debt. The only way this can be paid off is through privatization, and the productiveness of the revived economy will provide in an orderly manner the resources needed to liquidate that huge debt.

Observations. How rich this nation has been can be clearly seen in that despite being born in bloody warfare and having paid for and suffered through, more bloody warfare--the Civil War, two World Wars and several lesser wars--the people of this nation guided by a unique structure of government became richer and wealthier than any others in history. But this terminated with the New Deal and the Great Society imposing a socialistic kind of government upon us, now being worsened by excesses in all of this.

Further, governments should not deal with morality and welfare; these belong to the people. Note Matthew chapter 20, verse 15: "Is it not lawful for me to do what I will with mine own? Is thine eye evil because I am good?"

CHAPTER TWENTY-FOUR

At Last! A Retirement Income System That Provides Both Social And Private Security

INTRODUCTION:

This is an outline for a retirement income system to replace Social Security. It presents an honest, sound and practical way to achieve a reasonable minimal level of income when we leave the active work force. Social Security was enacted in 1935. A participant since 1936, I have been critical of it from the start. Now having witnessed its degeneration, I feel it is my duty to produce this paper. It is a preliminary attempt and will require much work to create a final draft.

PREFACE - A BALANCED WORLD:

This nation needs a new philosophy of balance of government and economy. Our people in their frequent strident and loud calls for a limit on debt and balanced budgets have already made it clear that it is what they want. But this is just the beginning.

This disparity in the private sector has been leading to class warfare, pushed op by the politicians. This must be stopped which can be only by permitting the private sector to function to its full potentials. This is simple to do, taking back the excessive powers of the government.

It is not too late. Now there is a great opportunity to take great steps in the right direction. They at the start will be compromising steps but-that always is required to obtain balance between conflicting forces.

Specifically, the major elements fomenting much of this imbalance are the so-called "entitlements", principally Social Security and Medicare, plus the Obamacare monster that is just starting to further upset the imbalance. Social Security will be addressed in this part. This failed and sick system is almost entirely the result of this imbalance, made worse by bad design and blind blunders in its administration. This desire and need for reasonable income after retirement from the work force can be obtained by scrapping the present sorry system and adopting a new, privatized, system along the lines recommended herein.

In this recommended system, the people will be given a chance to provide for their own, but it will still at the start require defined government assistance. It calls for the smooth diversion of the revenues from income tax directly to the participants, which will require new sources for revenues to replace them, ideally those that will not increase the overall level of income tax revenus--i.e., no increase in those taxes. Again, a balancing process.

This country suffers from overconsumption, consuming more than it produces. We have become a debtor nation. This is a crisis situation that must be corrected. The major cause is so-called entitlement spending. In both Social Security and Medicare, benefits have been increased without the means to pay for them.

In other major areas the government has also aggressively pushed and activated similar short-sighted policies. Restrictive regulations and punitive taxes have not only increased cost of production but also withheld the available resources from being used. This is particularly obvious in the area of energy. Even such unproven fantasies as global warming are being used, all of which devastate current production.

A government that aggressively promotes restrictions on production is a government that leads to impoverishment. That some people have more than other people is not to be blamed on certain people and their greed when it is obviously the fault of a short-sighted government reducing the wherewithal of all, the rich, the middle class and the poor. This conclusion requires only logic and common sense, not expertise in economics. All of these are obviously major areas needing major efforts to restore at least some semblance of balance.

In this country's founding, its objectives were defined simply: Life, Liberty and the Pursuit of Happiness (well-being, i.e.). There was also part of the basic philosophy in it for these benefits to be shared equally and fairly by all citizens.

BASIC ASSUMPTIONS

The constructive and sound assumptions underlying this proposed plan for retirement income (that for health care to follow) are simply that by eliminating big government and the slide to socialism, we will be on the path not only restore individual freedom but also renewed prosperity for this country. For lack of better alternatives, we should look to the free market for a turnaround.

The features recommended are intended to be completely compatible and in furtherance of the objectives above stated. People will again have both opportunities and responsibilities now absent in working towards these ends. It faces up to the huge debt, both acknowledged and that not (several times our GDP) we now have and which ultimately must be paid by the taxpayers in the private sector, a lengthy process but the only honest way short of virtual default. With the people again having confidence that we are heading in the right direction, they will have the patience and resolve to move this huge mountain. The economic as well as the moral and ethical forces will work together to reach the results the people want in a reasonable period.

ELEMENTS OF THE RETIREMENT INCOME PLAN

Each participant must be an American citizen. Participation is voluntary. Each participant must file an annual Federal income tax return with a special retirement income schedule.

Participation at the start will consist of three groups:

Group A. Those at ages 25 to 44 when the plan starts. Their participation as a contributor will start when they first receive taxable compensation.

Group B. Those ages 45 to 54 when the plan starts. Their participation as a contributor will start when they first receive taxable compensation.

Group C. Those ages 55 -65 when the plan starts. Their participation as a contributor will start when they first receive taxable compensation.

Contributions. All participants will contribute at a trial rate of 8% of their compensation, with a cap of $120,000.

Benefits. Those in Groups A and B will have title to their personal retirement accounts, and the corpus in the account will become available to them when they leave the active work force, which can voluntarily continue until reaching age 75. When the corpus becomes available, they will also have the option of merging it with a similar health care private plan. For those in Group C their benefits will be set at the same level now payable under present Social Security, whereupon they will transfer the corpus to the present Social Security Fund. But they will also have the choice of keeping the corpus and waiving the present Social Security benefits, with the further option of remaining in the active work forces until age 75.

Disability. Total disability will be the same as retiring from the active work force. Insurance premiums paid for this will be chargeable to corpus. Partial disability will be covered under the privatized health plan.

Death benefits. As the corpus is owned outright by the participants, the corpus will be part of their estate at death.

LEGAL BASIS AND INCOME TAX TREATMENT

The legal basis will be Code Section 401, adding new sections which for convenience will be designated herein as 401-R (for retirement income,) and 401-H (for health). All employee contributions will be from pre-tax compensation, i.e., they will be exempted from worker's personal income tax on this. The income earned on the corpus of 401-R will be exempted from income tax as will all benefits withdrawn, where proper.

THE FUNDING OF THESE PRIVATE ACCOUNTS.
GOVERNMENT AID

Funding, in the trial phase, will consist of the 8% of taxable compensation, transmitted by the employer directly to the participants account or where not employed directly by the participant. *Secondly*, the employer's matching contribution (6.20% for the retirement income) will be phased out over the first seven years of the plan-- 6.2, 5.0, 4.0, 3.0, 2.0, 1.0, and 0.00. The employer will send them directly to the Social Security Fund, and need not be identified by employee. *Thirdly*, the voucher plan (see below) of supplemental contributions to individual accounts (in recognition that these should have been invested in a SS trust fund but were not.) Tables will be part of the plan, with amounts the various participants will be eligible le to receive. This would be on a rather progressive scale, favoring the lower levels based on compensation. These funds would come from the government's operational revenues (in recognition of its failures to invest.) The government vouchers would be paid to the individual accounts in two ways: directly, based on the Form 1040, schedule R-1, or at the choice of the filer, by deducting the calculated amount from the income taxes otherwise payable (plus, perhaps, a small, say 2%, "bonus" for the savings in governmental paperwork when paid this way.) These payments would be coordinated with the IRS's regular procedures in making repayment of over collected amounts. The IRS would be given the responsibility of auditing the 401-R account when it audits the 1040's, etc.

When the plan is announced the public will immediately compare the possible level of benefits in dollar terms with those being paid by Social Security, but it is meaningless to compare those because of their uncertainty. In this evaluation, I present some rough calculations of what they might be. The largest variable is that of the investment climate. If we project based on what we have seen over the past 100 years, with recurring boom-and-bust business cycles, we cannot be optimistic. But with the privatization of retirement income and health care, and our people continuing to demand substantial reductions in government spending, plus the general recognition that the government must take major deregulatory steps to permit the free market to operate, then we can realistically project a very successful system.

As part of these projections, I have used a base yield on investments of four percent (4.0%). This is fully in line with what can be expected from a balanced, moderate-risk investment portfolio. Of course, participants will range from the poor to the rich, and the beauty of privatization is that the individual can follow those investment principles with which he is comfortable. Also, for the benefits to provide purchasing power, the yield must be sufficient to offset the rate of inflation through these years. Here, too, I am optimistic that inflation can be held closer to one percent than the three-plus we have been averaging.

But, starting from scratch and with a very minor balance in the Social Security Fund now available, it is readily apparent that at the assumed 8.0 % contributory rate and the employers matching contributions phasing out in seven years, there will be a chronic need for substantial additional revenues.

Simple justice calls for our government to return to us the Social Security money taken from us with which it has absconded (several hundred trillion, without interest), but this Ponzi-Madoff government cannot even pay its current bills! And unfortunately the government is us and we are the government. All of us now must pay the penalty for permitting the government to do this to us. Almost all of the funds needed for the new plan must be provided prospectively. With the employers matching 6.20% out, there will be only 8.0% from participants, only 1.8% more than in the past.

But there are these factors to consider. Unlike the past, there will be invested funds yielding, say 4%. Another substantial factor is the big boost to production, with its dividends, that the reduced levy on employers will produce over time. With the sum of the two, 12.0%, this should be sufficient.

But with this large deficit looming, where should we look for additional government revenues? I am proposing a combined national sales tax of 10% of which the federal government will retain 3%, and return the balance to the states; this would provide much needed standardization and would capture the interstate sales that now escape taxation. The standardization would include the definition of exemptions which are now too broad and have no consistent validation. Where the state tax is less than 7% the difference would be returned to the states for their use.

To determine the possibility that this 3% national sales tax might cover the voucher liability, I have made the following calculations and projections, with these assumptions:

- The annual voucher payments will average $3,000 per participants of which one-half would be paid direct and the other half by the income-tax offset.

- That a national sales tax be passed as outlined above, of which the Federal portion of 3% would go directly to help-cover the funding of the new retirement income plan, and that the reformed and standardized sales tax laws would increase the gross by 10% over the present level.

- Those projections of data for Palm Beach County, Fl under normal conditions would also validly apply to the entire nation. This data is: Population of Palm Beach County - 1,320,000. Annual taxable sales - $30 billion.

- Calculations: Taxable sales per person (rounded) - $23,000

- National tax @ 10% - $2,300.

- The Fed's portion @ 3% - $ 690 x 110% = $759.

But this $759 would go exclusively to the new retirement income plan, whose numbers should approximate one-third of the total population, so the $759 going to each would be tripled = $2,277. This is over 75% of the $3,000 voucher amount needed, so only 25% more of tax revenues from other sources would be needed. Increasing the Federal levy to 4% would be over the $ 3,000 needed.

Observation: Without the economic effects of the elimination of the employers match, the new plan would not be possible. It would pull itself up by its own bootstraps.

THREE EXAMPLES

Using the Appendix A table data, gives these approximations, all assuming the 4% yield has been achieved.

(1) Person with 20 years to go before leaving the active work force with average compensation of $50,000.

> Corpus at retirement date $145,000
> Life annuity with 4% yield $11,000-$12,000.

(2) Person with 35 years to go before leaving the active work force with average compensation of $25,000.

Corpus at retirement date $265,000
Life annuity with 4% yield $21,000-$23,000

(3) Person with 30 years to go before leaving active work force, with average compensation of $35,000.

Corpus at retirement date $250,000
Life annuity with 4% yield $19,000-$20,000.

In these examples as per the new plan there is no fixed retirement date, and participants can continue making contributions as part of the active work force' until reaching age 75. That provides in individual cases the opportunity to continue these tax-advantaged contributions, building up the corpus.

OUR FEDERAL INCOME TAX. COMPLETE REFORM MANDATORY

Reform in the Code. Amendment XVI, passed in 1913, gave Congress the power to collect taxes "on income from whatever source derived", without further qualifications. Ignored and corrupted ever since is what "income" really means and was intended. Unquestionably, this means income as 'defined by solid economics. Deduction, accordingly, must be only those incurred in the production of income, but due to legislative largesse and politics they have been expanded broadly and many for social purposes. In any reformation, these extra-legal deductions must be closely scrutinized and limited substantially. That of itself will greatly reduce the size and complexity of the present code.

There are established principles for acceptable taxation, and that philosophy should be followed. In essence, they say that everybody should pay some taxes. Further that the level of taxes on the individual should generally reflect the benefits the individual receives from the government and his ability to pay, which implies a modest degree of progressively on its impact. There are other practical considerations such as the simple, common-sense one that taxes once correctly calculated should not have to be redone on some other basis. The alternate minimum tax is an outrage and should be eliminated from the start. The 3% (net) national sales tax would mean everybody would be paying some tax.

The administration of the "mechanics" of determining taxable income and its reporting and collection are very important. Considerations here are covered in the following section, including the relationship of those "mechanics" and how they can be coordinated with the suggested new retirement income plan.

THE NEVER-NEVER LAND OF ESTIMATING TAXABLE INCOME AND THE COST AND INEFFICIENCIES OF THE PRESENT WITHHOLDING SYSTEM.

Starting in 1943, the government, in response to the need to speed tax revenues as part of the war effort, adopted a requirement to withhold personal income before legally due. Though "temporary," this practice continues today. Today, the zeal with which the Federal government collects taxes is a violation of our rights. This includes the burden put on employers and other third parties to collect taxes on income (even before the fact of taxable income has been determined) and forward it to the government. A mammoth chaos of estimating and withholding taxes has emerged, deeply imbedded and costly in its administration.

Federal income taxes are based on income for a 12-month period (i.e. "annually"). But we are required to pay taxes on this undefined, in fact hypothetical, income starting on April 15, inconveniently the date the taxes on the previous year are first legally due. But the taxes legally due cannot be determined until the income for the entire year is determined, which the law does not really require to be determined until a year later! And during the year further returns of estimated taxes must be made on irregular dates, June 15, September 15 and January 15 of the following year, which is still ahead of a reasonable date by which the taxes due can be determined. The penalty for underpayment of these hypothetical taxes is relatively mild, as it should be. And this can be avoided by making certain the estimated taxes paid equal to 90%, 100%, and 110% (varies by individuals) of the taxes paid in the previous year--- a very arbitrary basis difficult to justify as incomes always vary from year to year.

The tax code thus asks each individual to calculate his taxable income months in advance, and then penalizes him for his failure. The estimated tax returns should be only three in number, giving more time for accuracy, which might be June 15, October 15, and January 15. Then there would be no need for a fourth quarter return as that would be the date the final tax is due.

The withholding well in advance of money for taxes also follows the same illogical pattern, with the parties withholding transmitting huge amounts every quarter which in the final determination are usually well in excess of the actual taxes due. It encourages this overpayment by permitting employees to file W-4s permitting withholding off over the required amounts. And unfortunately unsophisticated persons, authorize this, rationalizing it on the basis that this forces them to save, which their lack of will power otherwise would not make them do. And these sums are repaid many months later, after April 15, and without interest.

The politicians would love enacting these benefits for their voters. And the employees having in hand the amounts they might otherwise over-withhold, would be inclined to actually save and get some current return on this.

Collateral changes and benefits from coordinating the above with the new retirement income law. With the new plan in effect after seven years there would be no more Social Security withholding for the employers to pay, thus saving them much paperwork and administrative effort. With the new system, all participants would be required to file income tax returns, which include the estimated income tax returns quarterly, as set forth above. The mandatory withholdings of income tax by the employers could very well be discontinued and the participants then would transmit directly to the IRS their estimated taxes as determined by the individual and not as now required by the government in set amounts. This would largely overcome the "voluntary" and mandated withholdings from the individuals and result in greater accuracy and eliminate the refund by months.

The penalty for not making the estimated payment required could then be very simply computed after the tax return for the year was filed by adding the estimated payments and if they did not constitute 75% of the final tax due, the deficiency would be subject to a reasonable penalty, which might be contested when the taxpayer files a report showing that was an unfair and incorrect assumption that he had actually realized 75% of his income in the first nine months.

RETIREMENT INCOME ACCOUNT KEPT BY THE PARTICIPANTS

In keeping with the philosophy of the new plan of individual freedom and responsibility, each participant will have the obligation of setting up and maintaining his own retirement account. In this, there are several ways for it to be handled. He can maintain it personally in an account "kept-by-hand" and appropriate to the long-term involved. Most likely, however, the participant will seek some help from institutions such as banks and trust companies, similar to those provided for 401(k), with the service fee chargeable to the account. These are, in essence, custodial trusts. The institutions here will have a great opportunity to also provide investment advisory and management services, also for chargeable fees. This new plan could be a very effective instrument in providing this huge flow of capital for economic growth.

This advisory service provided by institutions could of course be long-term, assisting the participants after leaving the active work force, helping decide how these funds could be prudently and prospectively handled, including assistance in such things as life-time annuities, which require expert assistance to be wisely purchased.

APPENDIX

50 U.S. Master Tax Guide. OTHER TAXES

¶ 47 Self-Employment Taxes. A tax of 15.3% is imposed on net earnings from self-employment. The rate consists of a 12.4% component for old-age, survivors, and disability insurance (OASDI) and a 2.9% component for Medicare. The OASDI rate (12.4%) applies to net earnings within the OASDI earnings base, which is

$97,500 for 2007 and $102,000 for 2008. The Medicare rate (2.9%) applies to all net earnings since there is no limit on the amount of earnings subject to the Medicare portion of the tax.

¶ 49 Social Security Taxes. *Social Security, Hospital Insurance.* A combined tax rate of 7.65% (6.2% for old-age, survivors, and disability insurance (OASDI) and 1.45% for hospital insurance (Medicare)) is imposed on both employer and employee. The OASDI rate (6.2%) applies to wages within the OASDI wage base, which is $97,500 for 2007 and $102,000 for 2008. The Medicare rate (1.45%) applies to all wages since there is no limit on the amount of earnings subject to the Medicare portion of the tax. Regarding household employees, any person who paid cash wages of $1,500 or more in 2007 and $1,600 or more in 2008 to any one household employee must withhold and pay social security and Medicare taxes.

Medicare Payments. Medicare Part B premiums ($93.50 per month for 2007 and $96.40 per month in 2008) qualify as deductible medical expenses. See ¶ 1019.

Unemployment Compensation. A tax rate of 6.2% is imposed on the first $7,000 of wages paid to a covered employee by an employer who employs one or more persons in covered employment in each of 20 days in a year, each day being in a different week, or who has a payroll for covered employment of at least $1,500 in a calendar quarter in the current or preceding calendar year. Because employers are allowed credits against the 6.2% FUTA rate through participation in state unemployment insurance laws, the net FUTA rate actually paid by most employers is 0.8% except when credit reductions are in effect in a state. The unemployment tax also applies to any person who paid total cash wages of $1,000 or more to a household employee during any calendar quarter in the current or preceding calendar year. For wages paid in 2007 and 2008, the FUTA rate remains at 6.2%.

FICA Tax Rates. Under the Federal Insurance Contributions Act, an employer is required to withhold social security taxes (including hospital insurance tax) from wages paid to an employee during the year and must also match the tax withheld from the employee's wages. For 2007, the combined tax rate is 7.65 percent, which consists of a 6.2 percent component for old-age, survivors, and disability insurance (OASDI) and a 1.45 percent component for hospital insurance (Medicare). The OASDI rate applies only to wages paid within an OASDI wage base ($97,500 in 2007 and $102,000 in 2008). There is no cap on wages subject to the Medicare tax (Code Secs. 3101, 3111 and 3121(a)).

FURTHER COMMENTS ON OUR PRESENT SYSTEM

OUR SOCIAL SECURITY SYSTEM: SEVENTY FIVE YEARS OF MISMANAGEMENT

Had a right-thinking U.S. government set up a retirement program, it would have devised something different than the Social Security system. The better system would have used private-sector standards of accounting. Instead, Congress and a series of administrations gave us a system that was dishonest from the start. It provided a huge flow of funds for expanding the federal government, funds that were illegally diverted from the true trust fund. It defrauded the people and gave them a false sense of security.

The history of Social Security is a classic story of a king who claims he can do no wrong while he commits gross crimes against his subjects. It is a history of a government constantly lying, inflating and imposing a huge fraud upon all of it citizens. This firmly establishes that it must be stopped at once. Even no system would be better! But a much more beneficial and honest system can be built through privatization. This chapter outlines such a system on a preliminary basis and that system plus privatization of health care on a comparable basis would completely turn around this country from the devastating direction in which it is clearly going.

Social Security has been correctly characterized as a Ponzi-Madoff scheme but it is actually much, much greater. Further, Ponzi and Madoff were more honest than our government! And we are all more gullible than were their victims. Ponzi and Madoff promised dollars in return, but the only fraud was not keeping the promise to invest the dollars received. In contrast, our government has taken dollars from us and our employers (or the sum of the two if self-employed) and promised dollars adjusted for inflation; it implied from the start that it would invest these dollars but never did.

Instead they illegally diverted them for purposes never authorized. Unlike Ponzi and Madoff, the government is not faced with running out of dollars because it exercises its power by printing money without any apparent limits. But the only thing that does is to make each dollar worth less; it does not increase wealth or our resources. We don't need S&P to downgrade our credit rating; our international trading partners have already done so, reducing the dollar to seventy-five cents!

This Federal fraud at its start in 1935 promised only moderate and essentially welfare benefits to cushion the effects of recessions. Now it promised a flow of funds, and assuring all that they are entitled to it. This might have worked but these funds were not invested in the economy. In fact, the government needed these funds as it was continually borrowing; treasury obligations would have been sound and safe investments. Through the years, benefits were irresponsibly increased as no provisions were made to fund these accruing liabilities. Cost-of-living increases were made and justified by the government's own system of built-in inflation. And when such pluses were not justified, the people complained that they were entitled to them!

These exactions without being invested naturally resulted in a system based on private capitalism not having the capital needed not only to cover current consumption but depriving the system of the capital it needed for growth. These substantial contributions by both employees and employers if invested would have been strong forces to make the system work and be sustainable; the absence of this carried the seeds of the system's own destruction. Our Social Security System became a system for socialistic forces that over time impoverish any economy.

The success of the system was further lessened by the unsympathetic income-tax treatment. Contributions were made out of after-tax compensation, but in recent years some of these benefits were taxed although income tax had already been paid on the contributions that gave rise to these benefits!

Under this inept system, the cost of labor was increased materially, adding to production costs, being less competitive, and higher prices. The out-sized benefits added to consumption while the system reduced the production needed to cover. Throughout this, the government showed it did not understand the working of a free-market, capitalistic system, while professing it did.

This fraudulent scheme became more unsound through the years. Yes, the government's crime exceeded that on Ponzi-Madoff. The government continues to reassure us in face of all of this by saying benefits are guaranteed because they are based on "the full faith and credit of the United Stares." But faith and credit without resources and an honest, functional government in place is just an empty phrase.

AARP AND SOCIAL SECURITY. THE AARP SHOWS ITS SENILITY.

In recent report to its members, the American Association of Retired Persons (AARP) begins this way: "Wondering about the future of Social Security? You're in good company. The program's finances have fueled a debate now raging in Washington. That debate often links Social Security to the ballooning federal deficit, although the program plays no direct role in the nation's debt and currently enjoys an enormous surplus." Its headline adds: "Yes, changes are needed to restore the program to long-term fiscal health. No, it's not hard to do."

This statement misleads AARP members, giving them false hopes that their money is safe. But we should not be too critical; too many other people have accepted this pie-in-the-sky, and most to be blamed are those in government who have the prime responsibility. The misrepresentations are twofold: 1) Social Security "currently enjoys an enormous surplus"; and 2) needed changes are "not hard to do."

The basic reason for this misunderstanding is that people are looking at Social Security on a cash-flow accounting basis, which can only see the present, whereas in the private sector all businesses look to the future, which in technical accounting terms calls for accrual accounting. We must recognize our debts and obligations which determine much of our cash flow for tomorrow and the future.

But in 2010 already on a cash-flow basis Social Security had run a deficit of over $1 trillion, and projections show no improvements. On an accrual basis, not a cash basis, of course, the situation is much worse. A reasonable approximation (I do not have the current report from the actuary of the Social Security Fund but have it for prior years) of the balance sheet today, would show $24 trillion for the present value of the promised benefits accrued, that being the total liability properly stated. Against that would be the assets of only $3 trillion cash and Treasury bonds, leaving accounts receivable from the U.S. of $21 trillion. This exceeds and is in addition to the acknowledged and publicized debt of $14.3 trillion.

The AARP report shows a chart until 2035 with estimated assets in the Funds, with the peak in 2020 of about $3.5 trillion now, increasing until 2020 but then going rapidly downhill. This picture is what it calls an "enormous surplus", forgetting entirely the unfunded debt of six or seven times that!

Its report on "money in" and money out" is quite interesting. Currently the money-in from some 80 million employees (and their employers) accounts for 81.9% of the total, interest on the Treasury bonds 15.0%, and income taxes on benefits of 3.1%. This 3.1 % comes from retirees who had already paid taxes on their compensation before going to Social Security. A double taxation!

The average benefit being paid is about $1,180 per month, $14,160 per year, and with this going to about 30 million retirees, amounts to over $400 trillion a year. With more baby boomers retiring, this obligation will continue to accelerate. Now *that* is truly "enormous!"

The possible "fixes" are ridiculously inconsistent with the basic plan, which was set up as insurance and so-called in FICA in 1935. The benefits are to be decreased (later retirement age) and the compensation to be taxed under a raised "cap" coming from people who will receive no additional benefits for their increased premium payments.

JUNIOR AS WELL AS SENIOR AMERICA
MUST BE CONSIDERED

Senior America. When this privatization plan is proposed, would AARP have the vision, courage and integrity to favor it?

Junior America. A-significant feature of this plan is that age 25 is the starting point for coverage. What effects would this have on "junior" America, i.e., those under 25?

It undoubtedly would have a significant and substantial effect, both economically and socially. A major effect would be on those industries employing many younger people such as fast-food chains, for they would have substantial reductions in costly record-keeping. It would also offset some of the negative effects of labor laws, etc. It would certainly help those trying to work their way through college, most likely giving them more work and less reliance on student aid loans.

It should also have beneficial effect on those graduating from college, with prospective employers readily recognizing this cost "subsidy." Also, when they do get jobs, it would be a big boost in getting them started. In my case, for example, after working my way through college I became employed as an instructor at Yale University and then as an auditor with Arthur Andersen & Co. before reaching age 25.

There are also possible collateral benefits. The impact of the first 6.2% of FICA might also lead to the exemption of the other 1.45%. It might also impact unemployment insurance taxes. The federal tax is paid by the employer but the state taxes, varying by state, usually tax the worker. Here the proposed plan might be the impetus for exempting the worker, eliminating the costly, inefficient withholding process.

Besides being practical, it would have much support in principle. In making revisions to the Internal Revenue Code, it might prompt favorable income tax treatment for those "juniors", giving them a head start before being hit by the blunt force of a lifetime of paying income taxes. It also could give work to otherwise marginal young workers, helping to keep them out of chronic troubles now ruining the lives of many.

CHAPTER TWENTY-FIVE

PRIVATIZATION OF LIFETIME HEALTH CARE

The present status of health care

Using the gospel of socialism, our big government has told us that we are incompetent and unable to take care of these things ourselves and then regulated and ruined our economy to the extent that we possibly could not take care of ourselves.

In April 2011, Michael D. Tanner of Cato Institute wrote:

Even under the Obama administration's most rosy scenario, Medicare is facing huge unfunded liabilities. It would have to be given at least $45 trillion now to cover all shortfalls for as far out as can reasonably be projected. And some estimates say it would take closer to $90 trillion. That shortfall cannot be fixed simply by making Medicare more efficient or eliminating "fraud, waste and abuse." Nor can we tax our way out of the problem.

The president essentially proposes that we continue to do what we have been doing and cut reimbursements to providers. That approach, though, has gone about as far as it can go. Medicare now reimburses hospitals and physicians only about 80% of their actual cost, meaning more and more physicians are refusing to accept Medicare patients.

Rep. Paul Ryan's proposal represents a different way out of the crisis. He would not touch Medicare for anyone on the program today or anyone getting close to retirement. No one would be thrown off of the program.

But younger workers would transition to a new system, one in which they have more control over the money that Medicare pays and therefore the decisions about what benefits they would receive. They would receive a subsidy from the government to help them purchase private health insurance. Lower income seniors and those with higher health care cost would receive a bigger subsidy. Seniors could combine the government subsidy with whatever they wish to spend of their own money to buy an insurance plan that has a cost and benefits that best meets their needs. Instead of a one-size-fits-all system, seniors would have many more choices than they have today.

Will it mean that in the future seniors will have to pay more of their own money or settle for a plan with fewer benefits, as Democrats have charge? Yes. But that is going to happen with or without Ryan's plan.

Medicare cannot simply continue to promise paying for everything for everyone when it doesn't have the money to do so. The question isn't whether future seniors will have to pay more or get less. It is whether those choices will be imposed on them from above or whether they will be empowered to make those decisions for themselves.

The official U.S. Government Medicare Handbook consists of 150 pages. The Affordable Care Act which is now in part effective has no official Handbook but should on be published it would consist of at least 500 pages. See Appendix A to this chapter.

The heavy tax cost imposed will be increased.

In a proper community concern for public health, the state is in the best position to address this. But why should the federal government play this overwhelming part in the personal lives of its people for health care? Obviously it should not, but for years it has, increasing year by year. Taxes (contributions) have become widespread and huge, and here are most of them.

Old-age survivors and disability insurance (OASD) (6.2%), hospital insurance (Medicare) (1.45%), with the total rate of 7.65% applied to payrolls, imposed on both employees and employers (total rate 15.3%). The 6.2% rate applies to wages up through a cap of $110,000. The medical rate, 1.45%, applies to all wages, without a cap. Medicare Part B premiums (for prescription drugs) a flat $96.40 per month in 2008. This is also collected from persons already retired by deducting it from their Social Security benefit payments!

In addition to these taxes, there is also that for unemployment compensation, imposing a tax rate of 6.2% credits against the 6.2% FU TA, rate through participation in state unemployment insurance laws, the net FUTA rate actually paid by most employers is 0.8%.

A common sense look at health insurance.

Prudent people are always aware of the risks that they face; they take reasonable steps to insulate themselves from them. For a very long time, private insurance companies have existed to meet the demand for underwriting these risks, providing these personal services at reasonable cost in a competitive environment by using probability theories, the law of large numbers and actuarial science. This has been done efficiently with a minimum of government regulation.

For starters, retirees drawing Social Security benefits should have those benefits reduced by means testing. A reduction would be made, based on the last income tax return filed by the retiree, but it is not based on tax payable but on adjusted gross income. If this be true insurance, means testing is out-of-order, plus the fact that benefits are already biased in favor of the lower end of the income scale. This gross inequity should be corrected.

A free relationship between the patient and his doctor constitutes a basic personal right, and the part of government here should be extremely limited. Ex-Medicare, the simple (and contractual) relationship was forthrightly carried out. The patient paid the doctor the agreed amount for the services and then submitted his claim to his insurance carrier. Today, these relationships are completely distorted. The doctor submits his claim, usually without the patient's signature, to Medicare for the amount he would like to get, knowing that the standard Medicare allowance is less. Medicare (and the supplemental insurer) pays with little or no additional verification. The patient is completely left out of the loop. Some additional paperwork could tighten that, but there is too much of this already.

The above should improve Medicare as presently practiced but, unless you prefer a Canadian-type system, there is one clear choice and that is to privatize health care (along with Social Security) into a coordinated, efficient system which would recognize the interests of individuals.

Entitlements vs. true insurance - Types of policies available

Politicians have been widely and loudly expressing the need for health insurance for everybody but in the process have been misrepresenting most of the picture. What in most cases they have termed insurance is not truly insurance but a process of redistributing wealth from the haves to the have-nots. This mandatory, broad-brushed policy forces all to be covered without reference to individual needs or situations. They are proposing "entitlements", not insurance. If we are truly to call any system "insurance" that term can only be properly applied where the potential, promised benefits are commensurate with the premiums paid, and it is voluntary.

We are faced with two major risks; dying too early and living too long. We can be insulated effectively from these risks through proper insurance coverage. The risk of dying has been very effectively covered in the private sector, with a minimum of government interference, by many insurance companies offering a variety of policies tailored to individual needs. But the risk of living too long and incurring rising health costs along the way can similarly be handled in the private sector by private insurance companies but here since 1935 the government has interfered and intruded.

For many years casualty insurance companies wrote a variety of policies covering health and accidents, tailored to the needs and measurable risks of the individual. But this was distorted and got off on a wrong foot during World War II, when wages were frozen and the federal government permitted employers to provide health insurance to their employees as nontaxable compensation. This was situation did not change after the war. It creates unfairness in income taxes as between those employees who receive such subsidies and those working for employers who do no provide it, including all those who have to buy it for themselves. All those not so covered, including non-workers, have to buy it if they wish to and recognize the need for it out of their after-tax income. Correction here is a basic matter of tax equity and fairness.

Health care reform is overdue

The present system is out of control. It is complicated, costly, inefficient, and undisciplined. For the benefits provided it is much too expensive, and is not efficient in providing the care really needed by the individual; he is now a number.

It would be best to toss it all out and start over, but it is now much too late particularly for those now approaching the end of their working careers. We must revive Medicare and keep much of it in place for them. But we can put in a workable system for younger generations. This chapter is to set forth the design of such a system.

Before putting in a reformed system, there are a few things that can and should be done at once. First of all, to establish tax equity and provide a platform for all, the tax-free fringe benefits now held by some employees but not everybody else, as described in the preceding section, should be repealed. Employers affected can make adjustments with their workers by increasing cash wages of the employees who most likely would welcome that.

Another plus for this change is that when employers buy group insurance for their employees there is a highly questionable savings. The benefits under such policies are based on what the employer thought are best for its employees but that does not at all correspond with what the employee would buy if obtaining an individual policy--"one-size-fits-all" does not apply. Had employees purchased insurance based on their individual needs, they most likely would have purchased different coverage at the same cost. Also, when employment is terminated, he is on his own, at an older age. There is also the psychological fact that the employees take this insurance as a "given" and still compare their cash wages with the market. "Deductibles" in group policies are not appropriate for all. As in most insurance, premium costs are lower with reasonable deductibles and lower co-payments.

I have not made a study of the present health insurance companies and what kinds of policies are generally available from them but there are a few basic things that potential purchasers should consider.

To the individual, concern over health like that over retirement and death is a lifelong problem, and the appropriate coverage should reflect this practical perspective. One-year contracts make no sense; insurance companies should be encouraged to issue, as a minimum, a ten-year term policy with a catastrophic rider and renewal provision. One authority points out the following:

Real health insurance would cover major expenses, not minor ones.

Real health insurance would be there when it is most needed--for major, long-term illnesses.

Real health insurance would be in force for long periods of time. It would reduce or eliminate "renewal risks." It would also give insurance providers a stake in the long-term health of the consumer to obtain appropriate checkups, exercise, etc.

True health insurance would be something like long-term catastrophic health insurance--there would be a high deductible and both the deductible and the coverage should span several years (i.e., carry-forwards.)

General outline of a privatized health care system

There is much similarity in my proposed privatized systems but that for health care by its very nature must be more complex. The financial corpus of both plans will be tax-advantaged savings accounts owned and contributed to by the participants. They perhaps would be established under a new section of the Internal Revenue Code which here for identification purposes will be designated 401(r) for retirement income and 401(h) for health care. As such, the Treasury Department will be involved in prescribing reasonable rules and parameters relative to the eligible contributions and withdrawals to conform to the plan as finally accepted.

What would be fair standards for contributions? At the start to give it some solid structure I am proposing as basic contributions the annual premium on a ten-year health insurance policy, in ten years ranges beginning at age 25, with reasonable coverage and deductibles. The premium would also include coverage for guaranteed renewal, of course at the high rate applicable to that age.

It should be noted, however, that these would be the standards; participants would not be required to buy such policies, but could buy other policies or none at all. Also, funds in these accounts could be used to purchase supplemental insurance such as for special risks (pre-existing conditions) or catastrophic insurance.

These rules for withdrawals would be proper expenditures for health care that are "ordinary and necessary", with the participants having the responsibility to justify their specifics on this would develop over time, like case law. But there is also some additional internal control in that these are the funds of the participants and they would be careful about spending them, and competition would be present.

After establishing the basic withdrawal amounts, there would have to be others to cover deductibles and other reasonable charges not covered by insurance, say, an additional 15 percent. As participation in the plan would commence at a set age (I have suggested 25) dependent children should be covered, with choices made by the parents. Of course there should be adjustments in the standards for male and female, plus also for race and ethnicity. All factors used by actuaries would have to be considered and adjustments made for them. Basically, the market would determine reasonable contribution rates.

To pin all of this down it will take the joint efforts of the Internal Revenue Service and the participating health insurance companies, including their actuaries. Their joint product would be detailed schedules for each class of contributor-participant, by age brackets and the other recognized variables. After this big job would be finished, it most likely will require a continuous effort by these parties to make the adjustments experience calls for.

The funding of the contributions. First of all, where the participants have taxable income (and like the plan for retirement income only individual returns will be accepted), this can be taken as a deduction of taxes payable, going directly into the account. (Note: This will not also be deductible from adjusted taxable income.) Then there must be funds coming from a government "voucher", in which the government recognizes and reimburses the participants for contributions (taxes) they have made for Medicare, which the government has misspent. There will also be a table on that giving a reasonable approximation of equity for each age bracket. And, finally, the participants can make contribution of their personal funds up to the limit for contributions.

The personal responsibilities of the participants in the implementation of the plan plus the yield to be expected on the corpus of the fund will be identical with those set forth for retirement income as set forth in the preceding chapter. There will be increased efficiencies because of the expanded nature of these operations and procedures.

There is another substantial benefit coming from privatization. As participants reach the end of their working lives and decide a quit working (and this would be individual, with no set official retirement age of 65 or other), they would make no more contributions to 401(r), and the balance in that account could be merged into 401(h), with consolidated reserves. They would also have the right to discontinue contributions to the health savings account. These consolidated reserves would then be available for the participants to spend as they wish; they own the account; upon death it is part of their estate. All of this might appear very complicated in comparison to the present system, but it is not.

The underlying and extremely positive effect on the economy resulting from this mass movement to privatization will come freely from the discontinuance of the taxes on the wages of employees and their employers' match. Instead of this huge flow of resources going to the government to expand its operations and dissipate it, they would be replaced by the trillions of dollars of investments coming from the participants and flowing most constructively into the private sector. Thus this country will have again the bounteous resources which will be needed to regain solvency and get it back on the right course.

In the funding of the privatized retirement income plan, I have proposed a national sales tax to be coordinated with the sales taxes imposed by the states (see Chapter Twenty-Four). This proposed an overall rate of 10%. This would be increased by, say, 2% to cover health care vouchers, but ultimately it might have to be a little higher to cover inflation and make it more equitable and fiscally sound. It should be noted here, however, that such a broad tax hitting the consumer would help restore the much-needed balance with production. All of this would produce during the lengthy transition a leaner nation, but it would be more fiscally solvent, its credit rating would be restored, and with privatization of our money and banking, the American dollar would be sounder than ever, a world leader.

A final note. Whereas for my proposed retirement income plan I was able to supply some reasonable examples of the quantitative results, I have not been able to do so for health care. I did, however, using reasonable data and estimates satisfy myself that my plan would be doable and successful when implemented. I attempted to get some cooperation and input from some of the big health insurance companies but they could not be bothered; they were too busy making big money from the monopoly here that big government has given them, and so they did not want to be diverted.

Some detail about the plan - Expected outcome

Each participant must be an American citizen and at least 25 years of age. Participation will be voluntary, and will be available to those employed and those not employed. Each participant must file an individual federal tax return, which will include a special schedule setting forth the balances and activities for the year of this special savings account. The starting date after age 25 will be the year in which taxable income is first reported, whereupon participation can be elected.

Throughout the participant's lifetime if he be reasonably healthy, there will be unexpended contributions each year, and their balances will be carried forward. At the same time, the corpus could be conservatively invested with a 4%f tax-free yield, being compounded every year, as qualified in the preceding chapter.

Exactly how much this might be is difficult to approximate until the detailed schedules referred to above for insurance premiums and voucher contributions have been set. But it is reasonable to expect looking at a person earning $50,000 - $60,000 per year through his working lifetime that will amount to a very substantial sum, the unexpended balances from which can continue to earn a 4% tax-free yield. And when this is merged with the retirement savings account balance, which will also continue to accrue at 4%, there should be a quite adequate fund to take care of the retirement and health needs of those people, to be used as they decide, until the end of their lives. And they will own it!

For those less affluent and less healthy, things as always will be difficult, but in earlier days most communities did a compassionate job of taking care of its own. As I recall my Illinois County had a "county poor farm" which performed admirably, where those able to work were employed there while living there to the extent able.

But that person at retirement will also be much better off because after privatization starts to yield its benefits the entire country will be much better off, with a reduced tax load and the growth that only the free-market can provide. And the remaining national debt will have been brought under control, lifted from the shoulders of children and grandchildren.

CHAPTER TWENTY-SIX

FURTHER THOUGHTS ON THE AFFORDABLE CARE ACT. WHY IT IS UNCONSTITUTIONAL

The constitutionality of Obamacare can and must be challenged again at the Supreme Court, and there are very sound reasons to support a challenge. In casting the deciding vote in the 5-4 decision upholding the law in June 2012, Chief Justice John Roberts argued, that it was a tax and therefore constitutional. While nominally correct, he failed to identify what kind of a tax he considered it to be. The income tax amendment made legal the imposition of a tax on income "from whatever source derived", and a person being required to pay a tax to personally take care of his own body rather than turning that care over to the government in the earning of his income should rightly be a, deduction from taxable income, and certainly not a taxable event! There must be some limit on what is to be taxed as income.

If it be a tax supported by Article I, Section 8 of the Constitution, all such federal levies "shall be uniform throughout the United States," but as it is imposed only on those who do not purchase the mandated insurance. Thus, the law does not qualify under this definition.

The requirement that citizens must purchase a product defies almost everything the Constitution says and stands for. We have a right to seek whatever means we feel is necessary to take care of our own health care. This is our freedom of contract. The federal government has no authority to overrule that. Moreover, the so-called "insurance" mandated by the Act does not constitute insurance at all, but a centralized set of requirements designed to usurp insurance.

PART 6

CHAPTER TWENTY-SEVEN

THE GOLD STANDARD.
THE GOLDEN FLEECE

July 25, 2012

To: Congressmen Boehner, McConnell, Paul, Ryan, Rubio

Subject: The Gold Standard. The Golden Fleece.

The enclosure is an inquiry into the causes of market failures.

Most market failures are caused by money failures. Governments feel they must manage the money, and in this they always fail because usually there is the exercise of power over principle, and often morality.

The trading market consists of equating values and then exchanging them. Except for barter, money is always part of this. Without it having a stable value there can be no stability in the performance of the market. Stability, of course, requires full faith and confidence in the value today and tomorrow.

This chapter discusses the value of the monetary unit and the universal desire that it has and retain that value over time. As history has shown, this cannot be achieved by tying in that value with the value of any commodity (such as gold) as there is never stability in the value of commodities.

The answer is clear. We must eliminate both commodities and government from the equation.

The stability in the price of monetary unit can only come from stability in its value. Markets set prices every day when competitive forces are at work among alternatives. If we could have a number of competing currencies then we could get real stability in the monetary units we use.

The conclusion from this as set forth herein is (1) commodities can never serve as the basis for monetary values, (2) the value of units can remain stable if true competition exists among them, and (3) the only role for government is to see that true competition exists.

In this chapter I outline a framework for a system of private money and private banking which, when implemented, can provide us the opportunity to grow and prosper like never before.

GOLD HAS LOST ITS GLITTER

A 24-CARAT GOODBYE TO THE GOLD STANDARD

Monetary economists cannot forget the gold standard. Neither can our politicians. They are still mesmerized by the thought of gold or some other commodity to serve as a stable monetary unit. They are searching for a holy grail that never was holy, and when it has been tried it has sinned against us.

The gold standard for too long has been the Golden Fleece of modern governments as was the fleece of gold placed by the mythical king of Colchis in a sacred grove where it was guarded by a dragon. Our Golden Fleece in Washington has been held sacred too long and has been guarded by both donkeys and elephants. And even the economists have been fleeced by it.

But what is missing from most of these well-intentioned efforts is failure to see that we have a too-powerful government exercising a stifling monopoly over our money and banking. In this the government has taken upon itself a great responsibility and at the same time claiming an adequate ability to manage and provide this vital fiscal service for business in both the private and public sector. Our administrations repeatedly have shown that they are not up to the job; they have not even defined "the job."

The number one problem then is to remove the monopoly, and the only way to do that is to assure and guarantee fair, free and open competition in this entire area in the private sector and this will automatically take place and flourish when the government is driven from the money temple. But then the problem becomes that of the private sector coming up with and accepting a stable monetary unit. The gross and widespread misconception of this/is that it must be a defined unit of some commodity, or even a basket of such commodities, with gold continuing to be the favorite top prospect.

In searching for a commodity standard, gold should be far down the list, showing great volatility and little stability. There is nothing in the current demand-supply formula that would indicate this would change. Its uniqueness in the minds of men has added to this volatility. We should have learned this from our history, where there has been no stability or consistent positions by our administrations about either how much gold should represent the standard unit or whether we should stay on it.

But what is shocking and more unbelievable is that everybody keeps looking for a physical standard whereas we need a value standard. Value has certain physical attributes but in the final analysis it is a concept, what is believed, accepted and measured in the mind; only in this way do we come up with the economic worth and desirability that we call value.

In late 2009 and early 2010 I wrote a series of papers based mostly on the reference attached proposing stabilization through privatization: "A Stable Monetary System At Last." In this I outlined in considerable detail a complete monetary-credit system with built-in stability because the market itself would control through adequate competition and quantity and quality controls as its fundamentals. In other words, I proposed a value standard that would be strongly supported by the market, that is, a "market monetary standard."

My papers were prompted by the Austrian School of economics who early recognized the need for a private, competitive system of money and banking to replace, or at least compete with, the government monopolies. Hayek around 1970 clearly saw and postulated the need for such a private system, but had nothing to offer. In the first of my papers, I said this: "Hayek came up with no outline of a system. He concluded "we must hope that some of the enterprising and intelligent financiers will soon begin to experiment with private monies... no senior banker who understands only the present banking system can really conceive how such a new system would work.... Hence, I think we will have to count on a few younger and more flexible brains to begin and show that competing private currencies are viable alternative to government monopoly of issuing money."

I took a broad look at the varied financial institutions and how they have fared during this present crisis. This clearly disclosed serious flaws in many. But the one that has appeared to I survive in fairly good order is the credit card issuers. I have concluded that this is the best approach and is the most promising, even after all the problems that might confront it when it spins off the appropriate facilities and functions so its members could morph into a special class of bank needed to activate the new system.

Earlier chapters addressed only the lesser part of the problem of privatizing our entire monetary system; it was directed at only the fiat currency party of it. In September 2009, after having received encouraging commentary from Professor Jeffrey R. Brown of the University of Illinois, I submitted those papers listed in references to Carnegie-Mellon University's Allan Meltzer, arguably for the last 30 years the nation's leading monetary economist.

In his kind letter of October 30, Professor Meltzer politely pointed out my gross omission. I had failed to consider the need for our banking to be privatized and how that might be done. He said: "I would welcome an end to the government monopoly on banking.

Years ago, I discussed this with Professor Hayek He recognized, as I do, that the most one could hope for would be the private banking system would exist side by side with the government monopoly..."

Despite the great challenge of proposing such a system, I set about doing just that. Using an approach consistent with principles set forth in Part I of this book, I ended up with six parts, as per the enclosed reference. This "new thinking" still remains a huge work in progress.

In further support of this, I look at history to see if such a system or parts of it might have been used in the past and are still being used. Here the Spring/Summer 2012 issue of the Cato Journal there is much encouragement. The issue is slightly undermined by frequent advocacy of the gold standard. Yet a number of articles stand out. One is "Where Is Private Note Issue Legal?," by William McBride and Kurt Schuler. They argue:

> *During the 18th and 19th centuries and for part of the 20th century, more than 60 countries had free banking. The major characteristic of free banking are competitive issue of notes (paper money) and deposits by commercial banks, low legal barriers to entry, little regulation unique to the industry, and no central control of reserves (the monetary base) within the national monetary system (Dowd 1992, White 1995). Among the countries that had a form of free banking was the United States. Even after the freest period of free banking ended, with the Civil War, banks continued to issue notes until the federal government effectively monopolized note issue in 1935.*

They later set forth this interesting information:

> *Free banking was replaced by systems of government mo-*
> *nopoly note issue, especially central banking, not generally*
> *because it performed poorly, but because it did not provide*
> *opportunities for monetary management and generating*
> *government revenue by creating inflation (Schuler 1992:*
> *30-39). The last historical case of free banking ended in*
> *South-West Africa (now Namibia) in 1962. There are,*
> *however, four places today that still have multiple local*
> *issuers of notes: Scotland, Northern Ireland, Hong Kong,*
> *and Macao.*

The second article is by former Texas Republican Congressman Ron Pau. A very sound monetary economist heavily influenced by Ludwig von Mises and Friedrich Hayek, Paul asked: "Why don't we denationalize money, legalize competition, allow free markets to work, and allow free-market banking to work?" In 1998, he introduced a bill to permit competition in currency. He concluded: "I think what we need to do is just restore the principle of liberty, defend our Constitution, and recognize that the government's legitimate function is to safeguard property rights and freedom of contract, so that the market can expand. The monetary issue would not be that major if we allowed some competition to come in, but we have a long way to go on that."

Professor Meltzer's position on the gold standard is well-known. Perhaps "the last hurrah" on the gold standard dates back to May 1982 to a debate between him and Alan Reynolds, sponsored by The Heritage Foundation. Meltzer prevailed, arguing:

"We face come serious and important problems. We should be discussing how we can get from where we are to where many of us would like to be—an economy with more growth and no inflation. The gold standard is not the best way, in my opinion, to get there. The gold standard is an idea whose time has passed."

The final article "Toward a Global Monetary Order" by Gerald O'Driscoll, an economist with the Dallas Federal Reserve Bank, offers a sweeping historical summary, but filled with generalities and circular reasoning:

My argument is simply that restoration of the gold (or other) commodity standard must be on the agenda for those wanting to restore a classical liberal order. Doing so undoubtedly requires greatly downsizing government. Downsizing government is its own imperative. A gold standard, by constraining central banks, would help limit the growth of government. It would also render possible a serious debate over the rationale for central banking.

Most revealing is this very interesting historical note:

In the United Kingdom for the period from resumption after the Napoleonic Wars to the eve of WWI, the price level was roughly unchanged. True long-run price stability is a major economic benefit of the gold standard. The deflationary episodes in the 19th century reflected the conflux of two events: extremely rapid economic growth and the international spread of the gold standard. As countries adopted gold, the monetary demand for it increased. Technological advances in gold production and new discoveries of gold eventually enabled the supply of gold to catch up to the new global demand for gold for monetary use (Friedman 1992: 112-13)

This tries to establish the merits of a gold standard based on the unusual and extraordinary event that during this period the demand for monetary supplies was balanced by "technological advances in gold production and new discoveries of gold eventually enabled the supply of gold to catch up to the new global demand for gold for monetary use."

The greed for gold and its fluctuating demand and supply situation can never make it a suitable trading unit in the market place. To give prices stability, the number and value of trading units must be balanced eventually against the goods and services being exchanged. These are market functions with the currency and credit values having to be in balance with the value of the goods and services being exchanged. Former Rep. Paul asks: "Why don't we denationalize money, legalize competition, allow free markets to work, and allow free-market banking to work?" While he is a long-time supporter of the gold standard, I am certainly in accord with him on this.

My interest in monetary theory and the gold standard goes back at least 65 years. After graduate work in economics at Yale, and then becoming a certified public accountant (1938), I read von Mises "Road to Serfdom" in 1945 while in the Navy, and then became a disciple of the Austrian school. I was fortunate in 1946 when I started to work for and with Philip M. McKenna and the company he founded, Kennametal Inc. He was not only a metallurgical genius but also a disciple of the Austrian school, and financed the first English translations of von Mises. He had strong Washington roots and connections, including Howard Buffett, father of Warren Buffett, who was a conservative congressman from

Nebraska who introduced a bill in the House in 1949 to place the country back on the gold standard. McKenna pushed this establishing the Gold Standard League, chairing it during the 1950's. For the final ten years of his life he cooled off on the gold standard perhaps by his continual reading of Hayek and the rapid growth of the business of Kennametal Inc., where I served as chief financial officer.

Perhaps the best of the three Cato Articles is "The Coming Field of Money Cataclysm and the Case for Gold" by Dowd, Hutchinson and Kerr. They write "A recurring theme in monetary history-is the conflict of trust and authority, the conflict between those who advocate a spontaneous monetary order determined by free exchange under the rule of law and those who want to meddle with the monetary system for their own ends." Indeed, it has been a battle between two different philosophies: (1) On monetary matters the government should have the authority to do what ever it likes, free from constraints of law or morality, or (2) Those who claim there should be a complete separation of government and monetary matters.

If we learn anything from history it is that the first school is unsustainable. This article also actually points out that for the United States to put its financial system on a sound long-term basis there must be more effective corporate governance of financial institutions even to the extent of personal liability of the shareholders and by the decisions makers, and the abolition of federal deposit insurance and over dependence on regulatory agencies which would rein in moral hazards, encouraging banks to lend conservatively and maintaining high levels of capital and liquidity, and the reform of accounting standards that are principle based, not the current plethora of thousands of pages of rules of current GAAP.

The new standards need to ensure that this correctly condemns the unwisely adopted IFRS accounting standards in 2006.

The most valuable contribution of this Cato article is that which the author made, as follows:

"Going well beyond such measures is the need for a new constitutional amendment that reflects the lessons to be learned, of which the key lesson is simply that governments and money don't mix. Central to this is therefore the need for a total separation of the state and the monetary and financial systems." This can be achieved only by a "free money" constitutional amendment. To quote Henry Holzer, writing in 1981, at the height of the last major U.S. inflation:

> *"To accomplish its purposes, that amendment cannot be a half-way measure. Either the government can possess monetary power, or it cannot - - and if it cannot, the constitutional amendment must sweep clean. The monetary powers delegated to Congress in the Constitution must be eliminated, and an express prohibition must be erected against any monetary role for government.*

"We would go further: this amendment should also prohibit government bailouts, government charted financial institution and government financial guarantees of any sort, including those associated with deposit insurance and pension schemes. This would help prevent the future reintroduction of deposit insurance and of new intergenerational Ponzi schemes such as government PAYGO pension schemes or unfunded commitments like the future Medicare. We would also recommend a balanced budget amendment to rule out future deficit finance: these reforms would force governments to live within their current means. We should heed Thomas Jefferson's advice, "To preserve our independence we must not let our ruler load us with perpetual debt."

Finally, the capstone of these articles is one which does not even have the gold standard in it title. This is "The Fed's Fatal Conceit", by John A. Allison. It is valuable because Allison has had a successful banking career and has taken his hard knocks. He worked for BB&T Bank for 38 years, becoming its Chairman and CEO, growing it from a small bank to the tenth largest financial institution in America. Retiring in 2010, he became chairman and CEO of the Cato Institute in June 2012, moving the institute in a more action-oriented direction.

Allison argues: "The recent financial crisis, ensuing recession and slow recovery were primarily caused by government policy. The Federal Reserve made some very bad monetary decisions that created a bubble, i.e., a massive malinvestment. The bubble ended up being focused in the housing market largely because of government affordable housing policies..." He aptly condemns FDIC insurance, which is used to justify many banking regulations and destroys market discipline in the banking system. Further "the intense focus from the regulators--particularly on Sarbanes-Oxley and the Patriot Act--dramatically misdirected risk management in the financial industry." We have seen the cost of regulations is huge, as costly as high taxation; without freedom in the markets returning there can be no real recovery.

He correctly criticizes the Fed for, among other things, playing yo-yo with interest rates, bad timing, inverted yield curves, and similar things that did not work. He handily disposes of the fiction that the Fed can set interest rates, pointing out that interest is a price, the price of credit, and price-fixing never works, with which we all agree. These actions have resulted in the redistribution of income from the savers to the borrowers.

Allison's reason that we must get rid of the Fed is that as long as the Fed exists, Congress will be unable to discipline itself. He concludes: "Like George Selgin (1988) and Larry White (1992), I'm for privatizing the banking system. I'm for getting rid of the Fed. I don't think private money can compete against the government… Although we can't get rid of the Fed overnight, I'm quite sure that the free market would choose a private banking system based on a gold standard."

Allison states that if we can't get rid of the Fed, then we should at least follow Milton Friedman's advice of limiting the growth of money to about three percent per year. We should end discretion and adopt a monetary rule until we can eliminate the Fed. But Friedman's suggestion is not a rule, it is a formula based on invalid assumptions about the behavior of the economy which is never that consistent. A Congress that can pass a "three percent per year" rule can also change it when it thinks it is politically expedient.

Conclusion:

Stability in monetary matters and thus price-level stability can never be attained through commodity standards and redeemability because there is never any stability in the value (price) of any commodity. Value is a concept and the value of the monetary unit is, after all, a concept. If we can establish the value of the monetary unit in the minds of the people, and competition keeps competing monetary units stable, then we will have the overall stability for which we have been searching and urgently need.

Free markets equate the value of goods and services offered for exchange with the value offered for them, whether expressed as money or barter. When money is involved, the value of the money is equated; it is the value of the money as accepted in the minds of the participants that makes the exchange possible. Thus it is the value of the monetary unit that is being accepted that moves the process. The fact that the monetary unit might be redeemed in a set quantity of a specified commodity is not at all relevant. Value is a concept; it is in the minds of the people.

The persistence of the thinking that the money unit must be redeemable to make the market function is a relic of an earlier age, is illogical and confusing. Governments have added to this in their lack of integrity in controlling the amount of fiat money issued. When excessive, we have inflation in the price level and deflation in the value of the unit. All this inhibits the free flow of trade, and adds to the distrusts of governments.

If we have free-market banking, with private banks providing their own monetary units, and they are in competition with like banks with their own unique currencies, then there will tend to be reasonable stability in these currencies. And this competition should also bring stability to the U.S. dollar. These banks would have to be managed to retain the full faith and confidence of the public. If they failed to do so, they would lose market position and could not survive. Thus, there would constantly be taking place corrective actions for each to retain that confidence.

In this competitive environment in the free market there should result stability in the value of these monetary units. This is what can be called "a market-value standard" monetary unite (or "a market-value monetary standard") needing no redeemability and requiring only limited governmental oversight. In this way

230

we can separate the government and monetary matters, and we would have quantitative and qualitative controls in place. That is the system of banks presented in considerable detail in the following chapter.

July 2012

Footnote:

The references in the foregoing by Allison to Larry Wright refers to Professor Lawrence H. Wright, Professor of Economics at George Mason University, who has an article in this issue of the Cato journal as well as in previous issues. They are informative but contribute nothing practical. They assure us that redeemability would tend to support the value of the dollar but give us no reason to think that the value of the commodity (gold) used as the standard would tend to be stable, nor any way in which it could be made stable. Nor does he give us any specifics on what the redeemability ratio should be, i.e., how much gold in it and at what value. Because the value of gold varies greatly over time, there would have to be (as there has been in this country's history) from time to time changes in the redeemability ratio. There would still exist this unacceptable dominance by government over monetary matters. Nor does the gold standard by itself balance the flow of money and credit and keep it in proportion to that needed by the market as it changes from time to time.

In all fairness to Milton Friedman, upon re-reading him I note that his 3-5 percent rule was suggested as a temporary expedient until something better comes along, joining Hayek some 20 years earlier in that hope.

REFERENCES

1. Hayek, Fredrich A. Denationalization of Money, Hobart Paper Special 70. London: Institute of Economic Affairs, 1976 (2nd extended 1978.)

2. Hayek's paper delivered in 1977 at a conference sponsored by the National Committee on Monetary Reform.

3. "The intellectuals and Socialism" by F.A. Hayek, reprinted in 1971 by the Institute for Humane Studies of a paper which first appeared in the U. of Chicago Law Review in 1949.

4. "Toward a Stable Monetary Policy ---Monetarism vs. the Gold Standard", a debate by the Heritage Foundation.

5. American Enterprise Institute for Public Policy Research publication of June 1983 "The Economist" on John Maynard Keynes 1883-1946.

6. "Men and Money". A newsletter of The Committee for Monetary Research & Education, of April 1984.

7. "Capitalism and Freedom", by Milton Friedman, a reprint published in 2002 by the University of Chicago Press.

8. "The Economy in Mind", by Warren T. Brookes, forward by George Gilder, published in 1982 by Universe Books, New York.

9. "Meltdown" by Thomas E. Woods Jr., Senior Fellow at the Ludwig von Mises Institute, forward by Ron Paul, published in 2009 by Regnery Publishing Inc.

10. The Cato Journal, Spring/Summer 2012.

11. My papers on "A Stable Monetary System At Last!", written in 2009 and 2010 consisted of six parts, as follows:

- A Stable Monetary System At Last!: Part I. Stabilization through privatization based on the Hayek-Heideman hypothesis.
- A Stable Monetary System at Last!: Part II
- A Stable Monetary System At Last!: Parts I,II and III.
- Our Monstrous Banking Monopoly. It is devastating. Is it Constitutional?
- The Moral Imperatives of the Free Market. The immorality of big government.
- The Serious Shortcomings of Socialistic Statism and Its Stagnation of Our Economy.

CHAPTER TWENTY-EIGHT

THE PRIVATIZATION OF AMERICA. A STABLE MONETARY SYSTEM AT LAST THROUGH PRIVATE MONEY AND PRIVATE BANKING

August 6, 2012

To: Congressmen Boehner, McConnell, Portman, Ryan, Rubio

Subject: A stable monetary system through the privatization of money and banking.

On July 25, I pointed out to you that commodity standards (including gold) cannot give us a stable system. Socialism sabotages our lives. We need a free market which needs the right financial tools to let it function.

As promised, here is a solid framework of a system of private currencies, credit and banking which when implemented will give us again the opportunity to grow and prosper like never before. Yes, it is a challenge to change our thinking entirely; radical and revolutionary changes require unusual efforts and will reward them.

Undoubtedly this will be greeted with skepticism and disbelief. But who of us living 50-60 years ago would have found it believable what we face today, with no solution in sight? This is an emergency and calls for very unusual responses.

This is not a centenarian's dream; this is down-to-earth reality. It is, I feel, my duty to take some strong actions to try and save this country that has been so great for me in many ways. My associates, knowing that I still have a very active brain and memory, have urged me to make these efforts feeling that my experience and my remaining talents would help.

Yes, this is a very right thing to do, to try and turn this country around and head it into a future of unlimited promises, which is what our Founders envisaged and covenanted for us. I am trying to keep that covenant.

A STABLE U.S. MONETARY SYSTEM AT LAST

THROUGH PRIVATE MONEY AND PRWATE BANKING

This country almost from its start has had a varied and turbulent history of money and banking, with perhaps too much democracy and freedom and too little in controls in the public interest. This history is summarized in Part Three, chapter 16, which concluded that this nation has here the major problem if we are ever again to eliminate constantly-recurring economic crises and depressions. It indicated the need for privatization of money and banking.

For over 60 years beginning with F.A. Hayek and the Austrian School many economists have been calling for the privatization of money and banking. They have seen that for the free market to flourish, this is a vital tool that is needed. Further, monetary stability requires stability in both the quality and quantity of currency and credit supplied to the economy.

In this country in the 50 years following the Civil War a relatively free market and economy existed and showed its sterling potentials. But this was purely an accident in history and was fortuitous. Many countries were then on the gold standard and worldwide the supply and demand for gold happened to approximate the monetary needs.

Although people in the western world from time immemorial have benefited from an innate trading culture, they have all suffered from the common delusion that governments are indispensable in providing efficient monetary media to facilitate their trading. This ancient thinking still persists. And our post-Civil War experience in many ways reinforced that idea.

Any objective review of what has happened here since shows that was no solution and, in fact, conditions have become worse. In the 100 years since the establishment of the Federal Reserve, there have been more and deeper problems with erratic business cycles, including depressions and recessions, than in previous 100 years. Our administrators have struggled mightily with these chaotic conditions, passing laws and attempting new control techniques, but they all failed. That is now being foolishly repeated. Our legislators are not smart enough to know that for free-market capitalism to flourish there must be free money and free banking.

In the private sector, monopolies during the past 100 years were recognized as bad, and legislation was passed to curb them with well-meaning fair trade laws being enacted but they have never been really enforced. But this country has never recognized that the government monopoly in money and banking that it has built up is perhaps a greater and more pervasive evil. By now it should have been made clear what is essential if we are to have a true free-market capitalistic economy.

Observation. The shrill siren of the socialists has been that we have tried free-market capitalism but it has failed us, and therefore we should try their brand of capitalism, which is, in effect that we should eat the eggs as the chickens lay them and not save any of them to be hatched to produce more chickens. Under this system, everybody should be happy because they are getting more eggs to eat. The truth is, of course, that the hybrid brand of capitalism we have been trying cannot efficiently function because we do not have the vital ingredients in our monetary system. Socialism is not a natural or voluntary culture; it can only exist when there is a dominant ruling bureaucracy, subjugating the people. They temporarily provide more material goods and ignore the immaterial which, after all, is what makes life worth living.

Yes, that is the scrambled soufflé of socialism.

The previous chapter pointed out that commodities can never serve as the basis for monetary standards, the value of monetary units can remain stable if true competition exists among them, and the only role for government in this is to see that true competition exists.

In the past several years I have done much research and reading of the leading economists and at the same time have despaired over the futile attempts of this country to get its economy working again. This effort has produced in considerable detail how such a privatized free monetary system can be structured and implemented. This is presented in the following, in summary form of the total which has six parts as set forth in the reference hereto.

I recognized that for the public to grasp, understand and accept such a radical and huge change in monetary matters it would require sponsorship by substantial financial institutions already widely used by the people in their every day lives in which they have confidence. Further, the implementation would have to be motivated by the profit motive.

The answer was quite obvious--the large and all-pervasive credit card companies! But they are all owned or affiliated with the mega-banks but these big banks lacked stability and when becoming too big to fail they have become wards of the government; in this close embrace of big government they have, wittingly or unwittingly, become part of a huge monetary monopoly, with all of the attendant evils of monopolies. This behemoth has failed us in the past and promises nothing better for the future.

But to have a monetary system it is readily apparent there must be a separation here--this part of the operations of the credit card companies must be let loose and made independent. The solution is to set up management-and-control entities that would operate a new system of free banks that would issue their own currency and credits in the same denominations, while at the same time getting the credit card companies to use such currencies. Credit card companies as they expand and grow and in their daily operations require huge amounts of capital, and they by sponsorship of this new system could "print-their-own-money" and acquire deposits, thus generating much capital. The answer was quite obvious--the large and all-pervasive credit card companies.

But as stated, all of the credit card companies are owned by or closely affiliated with our mega-banks. And history continues to show us that these big banks have no stability and have to be bailed out by the government. In effect, they have become wards of the government and join with it in a huge monetary monopoly. Accordingly, these credit card companies can be used only if they can be persuaded in their best self-interest to sponsor such new banks, largely owned by the public, which would issue their own currency and engage in banking using these currencies.

As stated these credit card companies are constantly in need of large amounts of capital to finance their operations and growth and this new, affiliated system of banks could readily supply a flow of capital. Accordingly, it would be in their best self-interest. Also, they face the constant and traditional enmity between debtors and creditors and could use some help in their public relations.

When the public begins to observe the benefits being received from this new system, it should create goodwill. The potential profitability and improved public relations would motivate them to proceed with setting up such a system. And once one credit card company started to move in this direction, the others would follow.

The foregoing explains the common-sense reasoning behind the structure of the new system I am proposing which as it prospers would finally give us privatized currency and banking. At the same time it would impose discipline on the U.S. dollar. When the government (and the politicians) perceive the need for the potential great benefits from this, they would be quickly move to act on it and pass enabling legislation. Required legislation would be complicated but with the advice of competent counsel to cope with the special and unique conditions, this should smoothly pass.

Following is reproduced in three pages an explanation and short summary of the final, six-part product. (See reference A). Following it are some ideas on the physical parts of the proposed system to facilitate its adoption. Also there are some necessary reforms needed and will be expedited by this new system, designed to finally separate government from currency and banking, and structuring these necessary financial service functions better to serve the free enterprise system.

Designation of currencies. Units of account. U$A.

Master Card, M$. Visa, V$. American Express, X$.

When a composite or mixture of currencies - U$A

The unit amount (value) of all currencies when set up should be 1 (one). It should have the same unit value as the U.S. dollar. Competition should keep these values the same.

For accounting and statistical work, the USA (or USA, like the Euro) can be used. It can be anticipated in time as the use of these currencies become universal, all of them might be designated the "USA". This could include the U.S. dollar.

As stated, when the new system becomes generally used and accepted and as their values remain the same, the same as the U.S. dollar, this might readily become the standard or universal dollar, and be designated the U$A. This would facilitate and make it readily useable in accounting, for national statistics, etc., and become the standard unit of account.

In coinage, the U.S. coinage could certainly be used, but as the melt-down value of any of them exceeds it value, the government would have to change the composition or it would result in a shortage.

Banking should regain its virginity. By law, banking should be limited to the traditional banking functions, including trust services. They should not be investment banks, operate mutual funds, act as brokers with membership on the exchanges, and should not engage in underwriting.

The market for seeking and granting credit should also be returned to its original functioning when borrowers and lender meet face to face and tailor their contract to economic reality; only in this way is the risk properly evaluated. Further, the grantor of the credit should also be required to service the credit. In this way it is the market that sets interest rates, and that would properly price the cost of the credit extended. (See below for comments on the Fed.)

In this way as the granting of credit would be based on an actual and realistic need for credit, there would arise no credit bubbles and spiraling of interest rates as the entire free-market process balances the extension of credit with the legitimate need, for it.

The present vicious cycle of closing smaller banks and turning them over to large banks, where the FDIC is used to cover losses to depositors, should be stopped. In most cases, the smaller community banks although doing a very commendable and quality job cannot compete with the larger banks because the present system favors and subsidizes larger banks. Thus, a sound and correct exercise of the credit-granting function is aborted, and the smaller communities are deprived of a quality service, all because of a bad system.

There are no real economies of scale in the banking industry. It might be noted that Sandy Weil, ex CEO of Citigroup who built that bank on the idea that in banking bigger is better, said on July 26, 2012, that he believes big banks should be broken up, and the consumer banking units should be split from riskier and larger investment banking units, thus shocking Wall Street. (I met Sandy Weil many years ago when he called on my company to solicit its business. I found him quite pragmatic.

The American Banker Magazine of November 9, 2012, carried an article by Louise Bennett which included: "Thanks to Dodd Frank, community banks are too small to survive. Politicians may lax lyrical on the importance of community banks to local economies, and regulators may claim the focus of their efforts is on institutions that are 'too big to fail', but the facts tell a different story."

We have seen that size enables banks to exercise monopoly powers. This has not been to the public good. But at certain points this bigness results in operating complexities and failures because they cannot be managed. Evidence of this is being seen frequently during theses present times. Even the accounting has not been able to keep up and does not produce meaningful and understandable financial statement, with the lauded "internal controls" being fantasies. Too big to fail has become too big to manage!

In this connection, this proposed system of private banking will be entirely dependent on correct and timely publishing of the financial statements to assure the active competition that is an essential of it. But this will require some substantial changes to correct for the government's inept and devastating interference into the art and practice of accounting--see chapter 22 on this.

When this new banking system becomes fully operational, there will be no need for the Federal Reserve System, and it should be terminated after liquidating its assets. But marking those down to market will result in so much red ink in its net worth that it will be truly terrifying and shocking.

Of course the Fed was a mistake. It never achieved the objectives for it set up by law--keep prices stable and promote full employment. It not only did not have sufficient powers but under the Constitution it could not have been granted such large powers. And in its fiscal functions, as John Allison has pointed out, it on balance did more damage than good. And it confused the people of this country by getting them to believe it could set market interest rates! Interest is the price of credit, and price fixing never works. And interest rates being a product of the supply and demand for credit vary with the quality and the times.

The duty and responsibilities of the Secretary of the Treasury then would be better defined, concentrating on the financial condition and status of our federal government. After the initial adjustments resulting from this radical change in this nations banking picture, and the economy responds to the better discharge of the monetary functions, the federal government would certainly be helped, making it more acceptable but still difficult in paying off the huge sovereign debt that has accumulated.

REFERENCE A.

A STABLE U.S. MONETARY SYSTEM AT LAST

An Explanation and Short Summary.

These three essays are a response to Friedrich Hayek's plea over 30 years ago for a stable monetary system, better than a gold or commodity standard as its basis. The ultimate, he said, would be a privatized and competitive system taking the place of the present government monopoly. History has shown that central banking is the major cause of credit instability and shortfalls.

Any proposed solution necessarily must be both complicated and practical and I have kept this in mind, basing it upon established financial institutions dedicated to restoring limited government and a free-market economy. In the present ideological atmosphere, that dedication will require much education and for that I look first to academia and then the public's ready recognition once it perceives its great benefits, not only individually but also to our entire economy, saving us from the stagnant socialistic future now facing us.

This proposed solution calls for enabling Federal legislation authorizing two special classes of national banks, entirely independent of the current national system. The first class, limited in number, would consist of currency-issuing banks (CIBs) that would also be authorized to engage strictly in traditional banking. The CIBs would sponsor and exercise structured well-defined oversight over a second class of banks (PBs) which would be an expanding chain of private banks. The PBs would engage in and be strictly limited to traditional banking functions. They would be relatively autonomous but in special situations where any of them might approach an un-healthy financial condition, its CIB would take over control.

All of these banks would incorporate and be based on the conventional fractional-reserve system designed, along with their basic structures, to assure the quality of the currencies and credits being issued, further strengthened by discipline and control over quantities of both being issued.

There would be free and open competition among these banks (and also with the existing national banks). That, supported by the transparency of their operations as published using professional accounting and auditing standards, discipline bank practices.

Through all of this, the dominance and discipline of this in the financial marketplaces would tend to keep in approximate balance the quantities of currencies and credits with the volume of market transactions requiring clearance. Discipline also would be forced upon the Federal government, with the present national banks being kept in line, and the actions and importance of the U.S. Treasury and the Federal Reserve System reduced and substantially reformed. The result might well be the end of monetary inflation.

Putting into effect such changes would require backing from the general population as well as from the financial community. Major credit card companies are the logical vehicles to push and participate in the efforts. But as they appear controlled by Wall Street, they would not be in the best position. The challenge is to get assets transferred to individual shareholders. Various devices could be used, including special public offerings. This would have widespread appeal. Accordingly, the enabling legislation should mandate individual holdings of at least a majority of the equity.

At least at the start, the CIBs should be limited in number to avoid the confusion of too many kinds of currencies; I have suggested not more than four or five. The new currencies would be in denomination and size conforming to present U.S. currency but be individually distinctive. The currency issued would be shown as liabilities on the balance sheets of the CIBs, along with the traditional banking liabilities, the total thereof to be kept in safe proportions to the bank's equity. This is the quantity control added to control quality.

The capital structures of the CIBs and the PBs will be of major importance as it will define their relationship as well as quality control. I propose it consist of Class A and Class B shares, with the

Class A shares being held by the new shareholders of the new PBs and all of the Class B shares would be owned by the CIB, with the number of B shares always exceeding the number of A shares. Only the A shares would have continuous voting rights but the charter would provide that when certain protective ratios and measures of capital and liquidity were exceeded, the B shares would then have voting rights, thus putting the CIB in control. Under normal conditions then the PBs would be independent, with their shares trading publicly but ownership restricted to individuals.

In the following I suggested some significant new benefits to the PB customers, using new types of credit-debit cards and other technological innovations that would be well-received by their customers and at the same time facilitate unique services to them and at the same time reduce the banks' costs and expenses.

It should also be noted that it is in the best long-time interest of the credit card industry to be more independent of the Federal government and "Wall Street", and to curry the good will and favor of the public. Over time with the accumulation of massive savings flowing into these private banks they would become logical and fertile sources to fill the expanding capital needs of a growing credit card industry. The industry should not be late or reluctant to note the mutuality of its interests with privatization as outlined in the foregoing.

Short Summary:

Through the sponsorship of major credit card companies, a limited number of currency-issuing private banks would be formed. Each such bank would establish a chain of private banks. Dealing in the new currencies, they would also do traditional banking. Although having much commonality, they would be independent and compete among themselves. Ownership of their publicly-traded shares would be restricted to individuals. The sponsoring credit card companies would have no equity in these special private banks but would recognize their mutuality of interests and there would be cooperation. The competitive discipline of the market place and the transparency and simplicity of their operations would assure the integrity and stability of these new institutions, thus promoting greatly the financial stability of the country.

The CIBs on their own then would have sufficient working capital to pay its initial operating expenses. It would then begin issuing its own currency, showing contra-liabilities for it on its balance sheet. It would also start regular banking functions, utilizing its own currency or U.S. dollars at the start. Also to assist in educating the public the sponsoring credit card company would buy that currency from its CIB and offer it to its creditors, perhaps at a small discount. Also, if new credit card holders would have cards using only the new currency they would receive preferential treatment at the start. Credit card creditors (vendors) would accept the new currency when induced to do so and when it became apparent it was as acceptable as the U.S. dollar.

PART 7

IMPLEMENTING PRIVATIZATION.

INTRODUCTION

THE RISE AND FALL OF THE AMERICAN REPUBLIC

Here is a story of decline in microcosm.

Let us assume that in the period 1770-1850 there would have been a southern colony-state consisting entirely of plantations with slaves and masters creating wealth by farming. When the farming was successful, the slaves and the masters shared bountifully in the wealth produced, and there was a surplus. This surplus then could be sold to other states and enough extra produced to plant the crops for the next season. They were also willing to give the state reimbursement for the part it had played in the production of this wealth. That was capitalism.

Assume the state taking five percent as taxes, but gradually through the years it was increased as the government became more greedy and those in power grasped for more power. But when it became more substantial to, say 30% to 40%, the slaves' share was first cut and then the masters' and both of them lost their motivation to produce. Ultimately, after much protest there will come revolt and revolution by all against the greedy government. By that time, most of the wealth of this state would have disappeared. Both slaves and masters had been starved.

Yes, this country has been on the road to serfdom, our wealth has been dropping and disappearing. Now is the time for revolt and revolution while we still have a little wealth left. This is no grim fairy tale. This is reality. History cannot be ignored. It is our best teacher.

This is a young country less than 250 years old. It has had a glorious and exceptional history--for its first 100 years. They were years when this country abided by its Constitution. Since then, however, our history has been much less than that. And the primary cause of is the movement away from the letter and spirit of the Constitution, which is a document for a free and independent people. It is time for the people to relearn the lessons of how the American Republic came to be.

CHAPTER TWENTY-NINE

What Faces Us .
The Hopes For Privatization And Resuscitation.
A Look At History Brings Optimism

As this country proceeds on it devastating course after the November 2012 election, it is important that we look back at history here and abroad to see what has happened in other countries with similar negative positions, and note what they did about it. This should encourage us to hitch up our britches and confront the future as constructively as possible.

Immediately following is a letter I sent to five Congressmen in June 2012, and its enclosure "Optimism After Obama. Confidence Comes Calling."

THE LETTER:

Optimism is not just a word; it is a state of mind. A positive. Pessimism is not just a word; it is a state of mind. A negative.

In the big government, socialistic world of Obama, freedom is given some by taking it from others. A negative. In the limited government, Constitutional world, freedom is given by granting it to all. A positive.

The world of Obama, with which he is content, is an international, incontinent world of conflict, filled with negatives. In the Constitutional world, the Republicans offer a clear contrast--a positive world of hope for the return of a prosperous and peaceful world. A clear positive.

President Obama, pushing on a string, thinks he can reduce unemployment, an impossibility. That can be done only by creating employment. And that can be done simply by removing the many restrictions that have been imposed on employment.

The unrealistic world of Obama wants exports only! We know we can't have exports without imports. That is called "free trade." It is truly free but the opposite is costly. We have been living in a country of excesses, followed by curses. We have clearly seen the excesses of excessive credit, with printing press money no cure.

We have seen the curses of excessive collective bargaining, where the power of unions supported by politicians and unfair labor laws has resulted in the loss of many jobs in industries trying to remain competitive. The results? Excessive imports of products containing much foreign labor; that was the curse that came home. Government forces the export of jobs.

All of this resulted in an excess of our consumption over our production for several decades--an economy out of balance. Only with the restoration of balance can we restore prosperity, and what is more, the equality of opportunity for all.

THE ENCLOSURE:

The election of Barack Obama as president in 2008 was the high water mark of this country's march toward socialism. Democratic and Republican administrations each bear a measure of blame for statist policies. Unrealistically taxes were cut while at the same time government obligations were increased. And this unwise pattern was also imposed on the private sector, with Congress encouraging people to invest in housing in excess of their ability to afford it, all encouraged by unwise extension of credit by the government. This was contagious; most states participated in the pitiful performance, incurring much debt. There was unsound credit, wall-o-wall, from governments and throughout the private sector. This calls for an accounting, and the time is now.

There is nothing more constructive and revealing than objective hindsight, and it is a virtue of a democracy such as ours that it has within its philosophical structure the mechanisms and will to correct its faults once they are seen. In our constant search for perfection, it is always looking for ways to eliminate its imperfections. In this partnership of people with their government, optimism and search for perfection are constantly present, reflecting the optimism of our Founder when writing the Constitution. James Madison acknowledged that in this free form kind of government errors were bound to be made, but he pointed out the hope that in such times we can rely on the common good sense of the people to correct things, and they would be diligent in their efforts.

Yes, history repeats itself, given a chance. We must be patient. The basic reason for this is man and his markets. Man is well meaning even in his imperfections and tries to correct them. All men are traders, constantly in the market to improve their daily existence in both material and immaterial ways, and throughout the world. Economists talk about discovering economic principles but they cannot and need not because it is the billions of people trading that really reveal what basic economic principles are. Governments make efforts to re-direct the energies of people here but their efforts are puny (and usually unrealistic) compared with the overall dominance of economic forces relentlessly driven by these billions of people.

It is because of the foregoing that I am motivated to look at history over the past 50- 60 years, and what was found was encouraging. In this I was greatly assisted by a recent article "That is then, this is now" by Michael Strauss, chief economist for Common Fund. Citing George Santayana's famous dictum, "Those who do not learn from history are doomed to repeat it," he argues we can gain valuable insight on how several major nations adapted to crises, for better or worse.

Though not a meritorious example, we can still learn things from Russia. In 1998, Russia was faced with a serious debt crisis by devaluing its currency by 70 percent, paying off its debt then with cheap money. This was dishonest, having the effect of defrauding creditors. But it reduced the cost of doing business in that country. Foreign investors and technicians were attracted to come in and capitalize on Russia's rich mineral resources, supplying oil to an energy hungry world. That country rebounded.

Closer to home, there is Canada. In 1994, government spending was more than 50 percent of its GDP, and adding the provincial government's debts, the total debt reached about 120 percent of GDP, about what our federal debt is today. When Canada lost its AAA credit rating, it responded with swift and dramatic actions. Strauss notes: "Spending was slashed. Taxes were raised. The government payroll was cut. Federal grants were reduced. Provinces were asked to co-invest in projects that required national funding. And the country's pension plan was adjusted. The final stroke was the establishment of a value-added consumption tax. Within five years by instituting the above program of spending cuts and tax increases, Canada had put its financial house in order. It is to be noted that this was precisely the combination that was rejected by the U.S. Congress in 2011."

Strauss also looked at Brazil. "In the late 1990s, when that country realized its government payroll was simply too high in relation to GDP... they made tough choices to dramatically cut government spending, including a cut in government employment." He added: "They incentivized retirement programs, motivating thousands of government employees to leave. And, within months after the exodus, Brazil began to get its fiscal house in order. Benefit programs for employees were restructured. The size of government was substantially reduced which, in turn, motivated foreign investment to help develop that country. What followed was the ongoing period of solid economic growth for Brazil."

Strauss is most instructive in his view of China. Even though under dictatorial rule it has been wise and responded to the needs and desires of its huge population. He offered this commentary:

> "In just a few short decades, China has moved from a largely isolated, agrarian society to an industrialized one that supplied cheap goods to the rest of the world--paralleling, to a degree, the U.S. Industrial Revolution of the latter 19th century.
>
> The industrialization of China created a massive middle class in the country, newly cosmopolitan and ready to engage in the great Western pastime: shopping. As a result, in the past several years, the slogan has been inverted Today, what the world makes, China is taking, in astonishing numbers.

> *Middle class growth and resulting discretionary spend-*
> *ing has not been seen on this scale since post-World War II*
> *America, when the U.S. established itself as the world's #1*
> *economy. And there is still plenty of room for China con-*
> *sumerism to run, simply due to the denominator effect of the*
> *country's population: 1.3 billion to the U.S.'s 300 million."*

Strauss might well have looked at Chile, which threw off the plunder of Pinochet's expanded government to move swiftly to democracy and prosperity. What is particularly significant is that it established the first and highly-successful, privatized Social Security System, a model we might well follow. Chile today has the top credit rating of all of the South American countries.

Strauss also might have looked to Germany following the fall of the wall and its unification. Faced with the reality of the Soviet-controlled East Germany, the pro-American West German government responded with free-market incentives following World War II, resisting what was going on in the rest of Europe in very marked contrast. They still have now a well-functioning economy.

Moving away from history, what encouraging signs can we see today? There are many but in one area there are surprising and strident calls for tax reform, asking for a complete change in the Internal Revenue Code. Most of this is directed at its complexity and administrative burden on the taxpayers, and there an industry has grown up to fill this acute need. The public readily sees the great variations in the income tax on people of great variations in economic income, and naturally call for "fairness." But most do not see the really devastating effect of this because it constantly withdraws massive productive resources from the economy and at the same time encourages and subsidizes consumption, perpetuating imbalance in our economy. It is constantly decapitalizing America.

There are three specifics here that are truly destructive:

1. Charitable and other social deductions from taxable income, greatly encouraged in the Code, but this not only reduces the tax load and revenue stream but diverts huge productive resources from the productive economy and also increases the consumption demands.

2. Without any social or legal reasons, the death tax also creates a huge disincentive for people to accumulate estates.

3. High taxes (the highest in the world) on the income of for-profit corporations which further diverts huge productive resources from supplying the needs of the people but also reduces the market for labor. And when these already-taxed profits are paid out as dividends, they are taxed again!

Any optimism about the reform of the Internal Revenue Code must be tempered by the magnitude of the problem and its direct impact on everyone; making it difficult to arrive at an acceptable Code Congress can pass. Here we must rely on the elusive hope that Congress in doing the job it should do will first, last and always keep its eye on the Constitution and its intent.

The Constitution's tax provisions are few and fairly specific. Article 1, Section 8 gives Congress the power to lay and collect taxes for the legitimate operations of a limited government of the United States, including its general welfare, (and not the general welfare of the people which fell within the rights and sovereignty of the states.) The Sixteenth Amendment further clarifies this by stating that government could also levy and collect taxes on the economic income of the people. This also modified what appeared to be the intended uniformity, and thus the federal taxes coming from each state need not be in direct proportion to its population.

But then the Congress beginning in 1913 used this amendment as the basis of imposing taxes directly on incomes from almost any source and for any reason it might wish, without limiting this to correctly-defined economic income. This expansion legislatively went into negative income, i.e., deductions from taxable income. Thus the Code became the wilderness it now is, not only a raiser of revenues but also an instrument to change the social structure of the country.

It should be noted that Congress in 1935 in getting into the social area enacted Social Security but the law was called the Federal Insurance Contributions Act, calling for contributions (not taxes) by the employees, with matching amounts by the employers, or if self-employed double the individual's contribution. This match is of doubtful legality as it requires the employer to pay an insurance premium on a policy where it is not even a named beneficiary; it also constitutes additional tax-free compensation to the employee. The basic fault here is that the Constitution does not authorize government to make anyone buy products (insurance) they may not want. Only a voluntary entitlement system would be Constitutional.

We also have optimism at the state levels. The American Legislative Exchange Council (ALEC) and similar organizations have been quite active and successful. ALEC for almost four decades has been actively engaged and the facilitator of good and limited government and liberty-orientated legislation in statehouses across the country. The recent successful efforts of Wisconsin Republican Governor Scott Walker are likewise encouraging.

Wisconsin Congressman Paul Ryan on June 22 spoke at the Reagan Presidential Library at which he said "Everything President Reagan was... optimistic, visionary and a bold leader.... President Obama isn't.... President Reagan knew in his bones that America's best day lay ahead of us... President Obama is content to preside over America's steady decline." Further, "What President Reagan understood is that the case for free enterprise is not just a material argument but a moral truth."

By contrast, President Obama has offered us a vision of big government able to satisfy the needs of all. Under the guise of fairness, his vision would take from the productive to promote equality. Evidence has shown at all times in history that this undermines the most productive and creative people. A nation suffers as a result. Obama occasionally may praise free enterprise, but his actions belie that support. The truth is he doesn't. There is no way that his health care reform law can be justified as an expression of a market economy. Over decades, this law may do more damage to the economy than any other enactment.

My search for optimism was strengthened in the December 3, 2012, issue of *National Review* in the form of an article by Kevin Williamson. The author argues:

> *Everything you think you know about the decline of
> the U.S. economy is wrong. The United States is today
> the world's largest manufacturer, as it long has been.
> Depending on whom you ask, the United States is either
> the world's largest exporter or the world's second-largest ex-
> porter. For all that dumb talk about the menace of "foreign*

oil," the United States is today a net exporter of petroleum products--we import a lot of cheap crude and export a lot of expensive fuel. The International Energy Agency projects that the United States will become the world's largest oil producer by 2017, surpassing Saudi Arabia. U.S. technology firms such as Apple and Google are the envy of the world--a world that sends its best and brightest to U.S. universities for the purpose of bringing them into contact with the innovative, entrepreneurial culture of which Apple and Google are emblems.

It should be noted, however, despite all of these positives, and they are substantial in adding to our GDP, the GDP has been stagnant while the population has been growing. It is clear that with all of these reasons for optimism, we must be pessimistic about the future unless this country wakes up and corrects all the grievous harms that our too-big government has inflicted upon us.

CHAPTER THIRTY

A COUNTRY IN REVERSE.
THE LIBERALS' 100-YEAR MARCH TO THE WELFARE STATE

This country for its first 150 years generally adhered to constitutional principle. But since then it has moved in the opposite direction. The federal government has forgotten that its powers are few and defined, not many and limitless. As a good example, one of the first powers was to establish and maintain post roads and post offices. With post roads, the Founders obviously meant the interstate roads, leaving to the states and the communities the duty of providing the lesser roads. But today the federal government has gone completely overboard, impacting almost every community, spending money and encouraging states to spend money they do not have.

Exhibit A for big government's mismanagement is our postal system. In this they have ignored that the mail is still the most important vehicle for interpersonal communications, but it has treated the postal system as an orphan child, letting it wander as it wishes. But the system, instead of breaking even, has had recurring deficits and congressional or Treasury bailouts. On the revenue side, the post office has failed to price its products as it should and constantly keeps changing prices "forever." An initial reform might be that in 2013 it will set the first-class rate at 50 cents for the first ounce and 25 cents for each ounce after that. Priority Mail should be maintained, priced competitively, and perhaps should have several weight-size rates. It is not the job of the postal system to subsidize commercial advertising, and for that mass of mail it should price it to make a modest profit, or at least break even.

On the expense side, there must be drastic changes for this is the major cause for the huge deficits. The system has a large labor content of moderately skilled persons, and the cost of that has been driven much too high, over market rates, by excessive unionism. As Ronald Reagan pointed out in the Air Traffic Controllers strike of 1981, public employees should not be permitted to have unions. In the postal system, they should be promptly barred and the existing unions eliminated, in the public interest. As we have looked to and relied upon the federal government as being the umpire in saying what is fair in collective bargaining, their judgment should not be questioned here.

These drastic moves by a government finally doing what it should have done long ago requires careful planning to avoid the impasse of a strike by the postal workers, which might (but should not) have much public support. In the meantime, however, the system should be hiring new, younger employees, denied union membership, and being paid fair market wages. If a substantial force of these are in place when a strike might be called, it would help moderate the effects and shorten the strike.

The government has also taken broad steps to do things that it has never been granted the power to do. The Constitution did not say that the government had the power to provide horses and carriages for its people, but in the General Motors case we have seen an outrageous extension of power in this direction. President Obama has said repeatedly that the government has saved the

American automobile industry, but this is false and an outright lie. The only "American" automobile company still existing is Ford, and it is not even mentioned by the President!

General Motors is no more; it was slaughtered and the legal interests of its shareholders and bondholders was stolen. And in the process the powers of the labor unions was kept in place and augmented! The tragedy of this is that it was those excessive powers that ruined General Motors and Chrysler. Chrysler is now foreign owned. And the "Government Motors" we have today is far from becoming a profitable company with the government having a major share of its equity. In mid-2012, the management wanting to get rid of the heavy-handed control of it suggested that the government publicly offer its substantial holding, but the government promptly turned that down, recognizing the mistake when the amount realized would have been less than 50 cents on the dollar! An obvious proof that the government had no place here. Instead our well-established bankruptcy law should have been used, with judicial review of the interests of all parties, plus what must be done to restore the economic vitality of the company. In the meantime, millions of Americans are happily riding around in automobiles made by profitable foreign companies.

The Constitution gives the federal government the power "to coin money, regulate the Value thereof, and of foreign coin." Although this was not granted exclusively, only the government now is exercising this power, and it has done very poorly and failed in carrying it out. This has a direct impact on the quality of credit extensions as they are always made in monetary terms, and this has been very shaky in both the private and public sectors. We have had a built-in inflation due to the instability of the dollar, and the public has accepted that if it remains below three percent per annum! And this very unsound credit-extending function has been a major cause of the big banks and other Wall Street institutions calling for government giant bailouts. They have been accorded monopoly powers and in the process of exploiting them, these institutions have become "too big to fail." Regulations without the needed sound stability of money have only acted as temporary life preservers and to repeat these financial crises.

We must also look back to 1913, when bankers, led by J.P. Morgan, established the Federal Reserve System. It was made an independent agency with the stated objectives of helping maintain price stability and to promote full employment. It has done neither, but has principally directed its futile effort to manipulate interest rates and thus credit to sustain a stable economy, without its chronic business cycles. Inevitably, it has lost its "independence" as set forth in a September 2012 editorial in the *Wall Street Journal*, written by John H. Cochrane of the Cato Institute:

> *"But the Fed has crossed a bright line. Open-market operations do not have direct fiscal consequences, or directly allocate credit. That was the price of the Fed's independence, allowing it to do one thing--conduct monetary policy without short-term political pressure. But an agency that allocates credit to specific markets and institutions, or buys assets that expose taxpayers to risks, cannot stay independent of elected, and accountable, officials"*

When we think of the Fed 10 years from now, on current trends, we're likely to think of it as a financial czar first, with monetary policy the boring backwater:"

And Bernanke continues with his hanky-panky. This was well summarized by ex-banker John A. Allison, now CEO of the Cato Institute, on November 1, 2012 *National Review* in its December

3, 2012, issue said: "Conservatives suffered a terrible defeat on November 6, and there is no point pretending otherwise. Republicans have lost the popular vote in five of the last six prudential elections. The most logical explanation for the pattern is that the Republican part is weak – and has been for a long time."

We are suffering severely from some Supreme Court decisions that are contrary to and in violation of the Constitution as correctly understood. One of the most harmful to the private sector was that they enlarged wrongly the rights of the government to impose any kind of controls and regulations the politicians wanted. As previously noted, the Writers had seen that some of the states had imposed restrictions upon citizens from adjoining states from doing business in their state. That was entirely disliked by the Writers who favored free trade among the states they were uniting. In the usage of the time when they wrote "regulate" they meant "to make regular." There can be shown no intent that they wanted government to engage in the regulation and control of private business.

Also as detailed in Part Four, the Supreme Court has been pedantic and narrow in its approach and has failed to perform the complete judicial function which it had been designated to do, thus to supply the flux needed to hold the whole together.

The private sector in its present desperate situation might very well raise such questions and start a war against the Court to review these wrong decisions. The Congressmen would be listening and then might join directly in the battle, with some of its first actions directed at the excess power being exercised by the president, and might not only repeal certain laws but also take from the presidency all of its administrative trappings and regulations that have severely impeded business.

In line with the foregoing and as set forth in earlier chapters which criticized strongly the administration of the income-tax amendment, if the Supreme Court were to regain its conscience and concentrate on exactly what that amendment said and acknowledge how it has been enlarged today, that would do wonders for the free-market actions of the private sector. Today, much productive resources are taken away through such tax regulations, wrong because it is not truly income. Corrections here would result in the healthy retention of these resources to be used productively by the private sector. And on the other side, there are too many deductions and exemptions in the income tax system.

Perhaps the most massive drains of resources today are the way the entitlements, principally retirement income and health care, have been handled, with the massive taxes on payrolls taking at once those resources from being invested in and going to the private sector, and this condition is worsening. As set forth herein, this might amount to as much as one-fourth of labor's productive resources! When these two entitlements are properly privatized, it not only will give the people back their rights and a sound economy. Control over these costs would be returned to the people.

Not to be forgotten is the part that our politicized federal government has played in promoting labor's share in production over the other factors thus making total production much, much smaller than it should and must be. The National Labor Relations Board does not have as its sole purpose (as it should have) that of assuring fair collective bargaining, but is an agency in place actively promoting solely the interests of labor, and has done so without hesitation to the extent that labor and therefore our total production has become largely noncompetitive in world markets. This change called for clearly on the grounds of fairness and the national interest is urgently called for and when presented on its merits should have little difficulty in passing.

There are many to be blamed for permitting these outrageous things to happen, all of which have contributed to our present economic and fiscal mess. The presidents have had excessive powers and in effect have passed laws without the previous passage by the Congress. The Supreme Court has failed in completely performing its designated functions.

If only a few of these urgently-needed corrections be made, the people of this nation would start to perceive what great benefits are to be achieved pursuing privatization to its ultimates. After privatization of retirement income and health care are put in place and operating, the people then might take big steps and call for the privatization of money and banking, with the credit function properly in place.

Even under optimum conditions, such extensive programs will require much time. Not only will these forward changes have to be made and this nation will have to recognize and admit the huge debts it has incurred with no plans in place to liquidate them. As described herein, the privatization programs suggested will gradually transfer to the private sector this debt, and it will stop growing. Instead of huge debts we will be building resources, but in the meantime there will be lean years, with consumption restricted to place it more closely in balance with production.

Patience and patriotism will be required. Privatization will be the support and provide the products that patience and patriotism will give us.

CHAPTER THIRTY-ONE

PRIVATIZATION THROUGH TRANSITIONAL STEPS. PATIENCE AND PATRIOTISM REQUIRED

A government dedicated to promoting the freedom of its people must possess within itself the freedom to act. But as set forth in the chapter, "The Poison of Excessive Partisanship," and elsewhere, our government now is in gridlock. Everybody agrees that positive steps must be taken promptly but in the struggle over power all principles have been forgotten.

The principal principles and objectives forgotten are those plainly in our Constitution, but tragically that document also has been forgotten. Our government has failed in its fiduciary duties and has directed the people to break the sacred contract the Constitution is today as strong as it was in 1787. Government cannot produce resources. It is needed only for security, and the private sector willingly provides the means to provide from its surplus. When it exceeds that, the security of all is endangered, and with that the failure of the private sector. With the freedom our government takes from the people, it also takes their sustenance. People are very unhappy.

Today, the people in their desperation are ready for action. The proper objectives for them as outlined herein are so complex with many parts that we cannot realistically expect that they can be achieved in a short period, but there are a number of transitional steps that can be taken which would be helpful in leading to the ultimate solution. Some of these are listed here.

To destroy the excessive partisanship my suggestion has been that the Republican and Democratic Parties be forbidden to operate at the federal level but be restricted to the states. As an alternative to this ideal solutions which might be achievable in the current political climate is the formation of a third major party, which would break the gridlock and have immense popular support. What gives this promise is the emergence of the non-party Tea Party, a huge group of independents who could readily form an independent party (which they might call "The Patriots Party.")

We are suffering severely from Supreme Court decisions that are contrary to and in violation of the Constitution as correctly understood. One of the most harmful to the private sector was that they enlarged wrongly the rights of the government to impose any kind of controls and regulations the politicians wanted. As previously noted, the Framers had seen that some of the states had imposed restrictions upon citizens from adjoining states from doing business in their state. That was entirely disliked by the Framers who favored free trade among the states they were uniting. In the usage of the time when they wrote "regulate" they meant "to make regular," i.e., to make proper. There can be shown no intent that they wanted the federal government to engage in the regulation and control of private business.

Also as detailed in Part Four, the Supreme Court has been pedantic and narrow in its approach and has failed to perform the complete judicial function which it had been designated to do, thus to supply the glue needed to hold the whole together. The justices had sworn to enforce the complete Constitution, and in its narrow decisions have failed to do that.

The private sector in its present desperate situation might very well raise such questions and start a war against the Court to review these wrong decisions. The Congressmen would be listening and then might join directly in the battle, with some of its first actions directed at the excess power being exercised by the president, and might not only repeal certain laws but also take from the presidency all of its administrative trappings and regulations that have severely impeded business.

In line with the foregoing and as set forth in earlier chapters which criticized strongly the administration of the income-tax amendment, if the Supreme Court were to regain its conscience and concentrate on exactly what that amendment said and acknowledge how it has been enlarged today, that would do wonders for the, free-market actions of the private sector. Today, much productive resources are taken away through such tax regulations, wrong because it is not truly income. Corrections here would result in the healthy retention of these resources to be used productively by the private sector.

And on the other side, there are too many deductions and exemptions from true income which result in it not being taxed at all. There we have massive sources of much-needed taxation, which legally and for fairness should be taxed. Adding these two gross errors together results in corrections that would be very beneficial in their effects on the private economy.

Perhaps the most massive drains of resources today are the way the entitlements, principally retirement income and health care, have been handled, with the massive taxes on payrolls taking at once those resources from being invested in and going to the private sector, and this condition is worsening. As set forth herein, this might amount to as much as one-fourth of labor's productive resources.

Not to be forgotten is the part that our politicized federal government has played in promoting labor's share in production over the other factors thus making total production much, much smaller than it should and must be. The National Labor Relations Board does not have as its sole purpose (as it should have) that of assuring fair collective bargaining, but is an agency in place actively promoting solely the interests of labor, and has done so without hesitation to the extent that labor and therefore our total production become largely noncompetitive in world markets. This change called for clearly on the grounds of fairness and the national interest is urgently called for and when presented on its merits should have little difficulty in passing.

As stated before, there are many reasons for this turn of events. The presidents have had excessive powers and in effect have passed laws without the previous passage by the Congress. The Supreme Court has failed in completely performing its designated functions. And engaged in bitter infighting, the Congress has failed to see these tragic things that have been happening.

If only a few of these urgently-needed corrections be made, the people of this nation would start to perceive what great benefits are to be achieved pursuing privatization to its ultimates. After privatization of retirement income and health care are put in place and operating, the people then might take big steps and call for the privatization of money and banking, with the credit function properly in place.

Even under optimum conditions, such extensive programs will require much time. Not only will these forward changes have to be made and this nation will have to recognize and admit the huge debts it has incurred with no plans in place to liquidate them. As described herein, the privatization programs suggested will gradually transfer to the private sector this debt, and it will stop growing. Instead of huge debts we will be building resources, but in the meantime there will be lean 'years, with consumption restricted to place it more closely in balance with production. But it will be a contented and happy nation, knowing it is at last on the right path. And the world may learn from our ways.

Patience and patriotism will be required. Privatization will be the support and provide the products that patience and patriotism will give us.

CHAPTER THIRTY-TWO

FINAL CHAPTER. A LETTER TO FOUR CONGRESSMEN FOLLOWING THE NOVEMBER 6 ELECTION

This letter was mailed on November 30, 2012.

To: Congressmen Boehner, McConnell, Rubio and Ryan

Subject: How high the cliff!

It is obvious that the people in government who are responsible for the worrying about the fiscal cliff upon which we are perched have no idea how many feet above sea level they are sitting. They talk about only some $15-16 trillion, of debt whereas it is closer to $60-$70 trillion, and that is the discounted present value of it, and it is growing!

The basic problem is that they know only cash-basis accounting but they should know very well that the real world is on the accrual basis, having to recognize that after the cash is all spent and there is debt remaining, the accounting has not been completed. But they keep talking about cutting taxes and balancing budgets! Even in their dream world they must recognize these debts must be paid and taxes are the only way to pay them. A budget is not balanced when there is debt left over.

All of us in the real world are yelling loudly, hoping all those politicians on the Potomac can hear us. If they do not have honesty and courage to confront the total problem, they deserve to float down the Potomac to the open sea. Then hopefully we will elect honest, straight-thinking statesmen who will face up to the big job awaiting them.

Among the Potomac prattle we hear are these. Let's forget about the entitlements and move on. But these make up more than 75 percent of the actual debt! Much chatter over tax rates. There are no magic's in tax rates; first we must confront what the taxes must cover. Ideally, we should be taxed based on how much benefit we get from the government and our relative ability to pay. But we have passed beyond idealism; this is the real world, and we must be practical. And the practical thing is to raise as much money as possible through taxation, and that requires much from everybody; there are not enough "rich" people to even make a dent in it.

The constipated Congressmen now talking talk only about income taxes, but there are also other taxes the federal government can constitutionally levy, and that includes a national sales tax. And there is very much to be said here and now that such taxes be imposed. It is the fault of all of us that we have been responsible for letting this mess happen, and we should be punished and have to pay for it, and that is the reason such taxes should be used. And such taxes will also cut down on consumption, helping to get that back into balance with our production, a chronic problem for several decades and getting worse.

Here is my suggestion. There should be a composite federal and state sales tax with a total rate of 10 to 12 percent, say, with the total sent by the collectors directly to Washington, whereupon the states would be sent back their designated share, and parameters would be set on that. This then would catch taxes on interstate sales, now largely avoided. It might also lead to greater uniformity in the determination of exempt sales.

With some 300 million people and thousands of businesses making taxable purchases, the gross revenues from this would be huge. The Congressional Budget Office could make calculations on this. Do you know of any better way to lower the height of the cliff?

This memorandum was enclosed.

MEMORANDUM

THE 2012 FISCAL IMPASSE (the "the cliff")

The fiscal "cliff" that we faced at the end of 2012, and resolved in a superficial way, is a convenient metaphor for collapse of governance. And what brought us to this cliff was an explosive growth in government spending and the taxes necessary to support it. This growth in government was a response to popular calls for entitlements, which, once granted, are politically difficult to remove. Retirement, health care and other expenditures began as "small" programs, but once instituted, have become impossible even to reduce, much less eliminate. Even "libertarians" in Congress walk lightly, lest they offend their constituents and lose their re-election bid.

This enables government at all levels, especially the federal government, to continue the deceptive practices that have brought us to this precipice. A federal sales tax or the years it will take to get this back in balance. Lean years, but we deserve them for permitting big government to get away with it.

The federal sales tax will do much to balance out consumption over production, in deficit for several decades. This plus the huge flow of funds from the people which will then be invested in our economy rather than being spent by the government, will quickly and strongly turn around the economy. These lean years from the sales tax will then turn into fat years when all of these positive forces under a free-market economy are put to work full time.

THIS IS MY PARTING MESSAGE.

This is less a book than a toolbox for our nation's official book, the Constitution. This is a challenge to the American people that they should welcome. Grasp these tools firmly and use them with much muscle. Great rewards will follow including Life, Liberty and Happiness, that for which we fought in 1776.